Somerset College of
Wellington P

Placements in Early Years Settings

Successful Placements in Early Years Settings

Edited by
Jo Basford and Elaine Hodson

LearningMatters

First published in 2011 by Learning Matters Ltd.

© 2011 Jo Basford, Lynne Clarke, Carolyn Davis, Nicky Hirst, Elaine Hodson, Karen Perry, Sue van Gaalen and Wendy Whittaker

British Library Cataloguing in Publication Data
A CIP record for this book is available from the British Library.

ISBN: 978 1 84445 382 5

This book is also available in the following ebook formats:
Adobe ebook ISBN: 978 1 84445 743 4
EPUB ebook ISBN: 978 1 84445 742 7
Kindle ISBN: 978 0 85725 012 4

The rights of Jo Basford, Lynne Clarke, Carolyn Davis, Nicky Hirst, Elaine Hodson, Karen Perry, Sue van Gaalen and Wendy Whittaker to be identified as Authors of this Work have been asserted by them in accordance with the Copyright, Designs and Patents Act 1988.

Cover design by Code 5
Text design by Bob Rowinski (Code 5)
Project management by Deer Park Productions, Tavistock
Typeset by Pantek Arts Ltd
Printed in Great Britain by Bell & Bain Ltd, Glasgow

Learning Matters Ltd
20 Cathedral Yard
Exeter EX1 1HB
Tel: 01392 215560
info@learningmatters.co.uk
www.learningmatters.co.uk

Mixed Sources
Product group from well-managed forests and other controlled sources
www.fsc.org Cert no. TT-COC-002769
© 1996 Forest Stewardship Council
FSC

Contents

Editors and contributors

Jo Basford

Jo Basford is a Senior Lecturer at Manchester Metropolitan University. She teaches on the Early Years and Childhood Studies degree and the Primary QTS programme. Jo has extensive experience in the Early Years field as a teacher, Local Authority consultant and High/Scope trainer. Jo is particularly interested in Early Years pedagogy and the role of documentation in supporting children's learning.

Lynne Clarke

Lynne Clarke is a Senior Lecturer in the Early Years and Childhood Studies Team at Manchester Metropolitan University and is Programme Leader for the Early Years Professional Status. Prior to that she has worked in a range of Early Years settings, taught on CACHE and PLA courses and worked for a local authority as an Early Years Consultant.

Carolyn Davis

Carolyn Davis is an Assistant Head Teacher with responsibility for the Early Years Foundation Stage and transition to Year One in an inner-city school in Manchester. Alongside many years of teaching in Foundation Stage and Key Stage One, she has also gained experience as an associate tutor and as a mentor and assessor in employment-based teacher training.

Nicky Hirst

Nicky Hirst is Senior Lecturer in Early Childhood Studies/Foundation Degree in Early Years Practice and Early Years Professional Status at Manchester Metropolitan University.

Elaine Hodson

Elaine Hodson is a Senior Lecturer at Manchester Metropolitan University. Having taught on a variety of ITT and CPD programmes she now works on the Employment-Based Routes into teaching. She has taught on Masters programmes for the Open University, and was previously a head teacher of a nursery school and then of a primary school.

Karen Perry

Karen Perry is a Senior Lecturer in Early Childhood Studies at Manchester Metropolitan University. Part of her role involves supporting EYPS students in their placement experience and lecturing on the Postgraduate Certificate in Early Childhood Studies. Prior to this, she was involved with Forest Schools in Shropshire, working directly with children in the Foundation Stage and supporting other professionals in setting up their own Forest School sites.

Sue van Gaalen

Sue van Gaalen has been a qualified teacher since 1979 and has taught in many different educational settings – both in mainstream and as the teacher in charge of a unit for children with Special Educational Needs. She has fostered more than 70 children and young people and has adopted 3, who are now adults.

Sue has been an Education Liaison Officer for an independent fostering agency, working as part of a multidisciplinary team alongside social workers, therapists and support workers and a member of Stockport's Education Support Team for looked-after children. She has been at Manchester Metropolitan University since 2002 where she is a Senior Lecturer in Early Years and Childhood Studies.

Wendy Whittaker

Wendy Whittaker worked as a Sure Start Programme Manager and Children's Centre manager before joining Manchester Metropolitan University. She completed her Masters degree at Leicester University (taught at Pen Green Research & Development base). Her research interests include the use of technology in Early Years, how children play and learn and multidisciplinary issues in work with children and families.

Introduction

Jo Basford and Elaine Hodson

This book is intended for all Early Years practitioners studying at undergraduate/graduate level. If you are required to undertake a placement in an Early Years setting, whether to gain a QTS, EYPS qualification, or if you are on an Early Childhood Studies programme which has a placement element, then you should find this book useful. Reference to the relevant QTS and EYP Standards are linked to each chapter.

During your university and college sessions, you will have covered a large number of aspects related to Early Years practice, including child development, pedagogical models and effective practice. Your placement experience is intended for you to put into practice what you have learnt. Yet the reality of what actually happens in an Early Years setting does not always match the rhetoric of what you have learnt or read about. We have included case studies, reflective and practical tasks in each chapter, and hope these will help you to reflect upon some of the tensions, challenges and dilemmas that practitioners experience. Some of these tensions are due to the nature of relationships which have been established in a setting, but there are also occasions when practitioners are grappling with implementing an approach that does not necessarily sit comfortably with their own beliefs and values. As an emerging professional, you too will find yourself in this situation. Therefore, we hope that this book provides you with opportunities to reflect on many aspects of practice, while anticipating your own professional development.

There are three key elements to the book.

1 An overview of the unique features of the range of Early Years settings in which students may be placed.

2 Guidance, support and reflection in relation to professional practice and conduct before, during and after the placement experience.

3 An understanding of how the themes and commitments underpinning the Early Years Foundation Stage (EYFS) are reflected in professional practice.

Chapter 1 –The range and diversity of Early Years settings provides an historical overview of the development of Early Years provision. It explores the unique features of settings within three specific contexts: the Private, Voluntary and Independent (PVI) sector; the School context; and multi-professional context.

Chapter 2 – Preparing for your placement guides you through this process. You are introduced to the theoretical models of reflective practice.

Chapter 3 – The placement experience builds on models of reflective practice and encourages you to consider your professional conduct, and in particular how you build and maintain professional relationships.

The following four chapters are concerned with the Early Years Foundation Stage Framework principles, themes and commitments, and are intended to help you understand in greater depth the way the principles of this framework are implemented in practice.

Chapter 4 – A unique child, is an exploration of effective practice concerned with supporting the individual needs of children. It also covers specific guidance concerning inclusive practice; health and safety; and child protection.

Chapter 5 – Positive relationships, specifically focuses on four key 'commitments' linked to this EYFS theme: working as a member of a team; working with parents; interactions and relationships with children; and the key person role.

Chapter 6 – Enabling environments looks specifically at Observation, Assessment and Planning. It also encourages you to consider how the learning environment supports children's learning as well as the 'wider context'.

Chapter 7 – Learning and development will help you support these areas for children in your care. It explores some key research in the area, discusses significant pedagogical issues, and focuses in particular on the role of the adult in early learning.

The final chapter of this book – *Chapter 8 – Next steps* encourages you to take a step back and evaluate your own learning journey during your placement. It takes an anticipatory approach, where you will consider the next steps for your professional development.

Working with young children demands passion, professionalism and commitment. Throughout your professional working life you will be privileged to share significant and wondrous moments of a child's learning and development. There will also, undoubtedly, be times when you are grappling with your own professional identity and beliefs. Sometimes this will be the result of the environment you are working in, but on other occasions the circumstances will be beyond your control. Nevertheless, we hope that this book provides you with a suitable starting point to becoming an effective and professional practitioner.

1 The range and diversity of Early Years settings

Jo Basford

CHAPTER OBJECTIVES

By the end of this chapter you should:

- *have an understanding of the historical development of Early Years provision;*
- *know about the range and diversity of Early Years settings available to children and families;*
- *have an awareness of some of the unique features of each type of Early Years provision.*

This chapter addresses the following Professional Standards for QTS and EYPS:
QTS: Q3; 5; 6; 15.
EYPS: S1; 4; 24; 29; 33.

Introduction

This chapter is intended to give you a detailed insight into the range of Early Years settings you may encounter during your placements. A child's access to a particular type of provision is usually dependent on a family's needs. For example, parents who both work may well require a setting which offers full day care. Alternatively, some children are cared for by their family members, and will access sessional care in order to develop their social skills, or to prepare them for full-time schooling.

Early Years settings tend to fall into two broad categories.

- Settings 'maintained' financially by the local authority (LA).

- Settings which receive funding from other sources. These settings are commonly referred to as the PVI sector (Private, Voluntary or Independently funded) or 'non-maintained'. (See Table 1.1.)

Maintained settings (Public/LA funding)	Non-maintained settings (funded from revenue other than LA)
School – Nursery class/ Reception class/ Foundation Unit (*term time only*).	Private/Independent – Day nursery (*up to 50 weeks per year*) or school (*term time only*) run by a company or individual owner.
Nursery school – staffing commensurate with a primary school, including a head teacher (*term time only*).	Voluntary – preschool or playgroup run by a voluntary or charitable group. For example the PLA, Barnardos, NSPCC or social enterprise. These are not-for-profit organisations (*usually only term time*).
Children's Centre – a multidisciplinary team (including a centre manager and teacher) employed by the LA (*sessional 'groups' and full-time day care*).	Children's Centre – the day care element may be delivered by a PVI provider (*up to 50 weeks per year*).
Family Centre – usually funded through Social Care budget (*sessions only offered to children and families as identified 'in need'*).	Childminder (*up to 50 weeks per year*).

Table 1.1 The range of settings available to families

It is important that you understand how and why there is such a diverse range of settings available for parents/carers to choose from. The political landscape over the last 40 years has transformed and influenced society's thinking about the needs of young children. This, in turn, has had a significant impact on the phenomenal growth within the Early Years sector. The first section of this chapter provides you with an overview of the way Early Years provision has evolved over time and considers the way government policy has influenced this growth. Understanding the sociological and political dimensions of policy and practice is an important area of your own professional development. The ability to critically reflect on, and to problematise some of the issues and tensions for practitioners within the Early Years field, will help you to understand the unique range of challenges practitioners face within their own provision. The remainder of this chapter outlines in more detail the unique features pertinent to the type of provision in which you may be placed.

The historical development of Early Years services

In pre-industrialised times, childcare was predominantly the woman's role. Mothers were expected to combine work and home. There was a great reliance on older siblings or the extended family to look after the younger children while mothers went out to work on the land. It was not uncommon practice for babies to be taken out to the fields with their mothers or for young children to participate, in a small scale, in cottage industries such as spinning and weaving, developing skills for their adult life.

Industrialisation had a significant impact on families, many of whom moved to the towns and cities to work in factories. Families no longer had access to their extended family, and older siblings were sent to work themselves in the factories and mills. Mothers had to rely on far less suitable care for their youngest, through either wet nurses or minding schools (commonly termed 'baby farms'). By the end of the nineteenth century, universal education had been introduced in order to purposefully occupy the youngest children who were unable to work. Large numbers of young children were forced into inappropriate formal learning conditions. Yet this was also the period of the enlightenment, and there was now a growing recognition of the need for young children to be nurtured and protected. Children under the age of five became excluded from the state system, and the care and education of these children was heavily reliant on such pioneers as Margaret McMillan and philanthropist mill owners such as Robert Owen who established nursery schools. Emphasis grew on the health and care of working-class children who were living in poor conditions. The expansion of nursery provision continued up to the Second World War, because of the demand for mothers in the labour force, and this practice continued. With the immense growth of provision, but very little money to provide suitable accommodation and an appropriately trained workforce, there was a need to regulate standards of childcare with the Nurseries and Childminders Regulation Act 1948.

Post-1945 provision

After the Second World War, the education and care of young children became traditionally separated. This separation rested not only on the type of provision available, but also reflected society's views concerning the responsibility for the care and education of young children. Mothers were no longer required to work and returned home to make way for the returning soldiers, and day nursery provision was reduced by half. Alongside this, views regarding the damaging effect of day care on children (Bowlby, 1958) led to the belief that children needed the constant presence of their mother.

Government thinking was that childcare was predominantly the responsibility of parents. The nature and type of settings, therefore, available to children and their families reflected this notion. Provision available was limited in scope, accessibility and quality, and heavily dependent on local communities (predominantly parents) establishing their own voluntary resources to meet the needs of the families in that area. State-funded settings such as Family Centres and nursery classes/nursery schools, since they were costly, were generally only available to families in areas of significant social and economic deprivation. By the 1980s there became an increasing emphasis on equality of provision for all children. The 1989 Children Act (part x) provided specific regulatory requirements for provision in the non-maintained sector and, in 1991, the DfES commissioned the report *Starting with Quality* (Rumbold Report). This marked the inception of changes to Early Years provision, which gathered momentum as the political landscape changed.

New Labour policies for children

In 1997, the Labour Party won the general election. The new government demonstrated a huge commitment not only to 'education, education, education', but also to the care, learning and development needs of young children. This was evident in its National Childcare Strategy (NCS) (DfEE, 1998). Baldock (2001) cites this commitment as a crucial shift in social policy, comparable in significance to the creation of the Welfare State which provided a National Health Service in the post-war years.

With the establishment of the NCS in 1998, and its three key aims of accessibility, afford-ability, and quality of childcare, came a significant focus on both increasing the number of Early Years places for children, and improving the standards of care and of education. OFSTED was given overall responsibility for this regulation of standards. In addition, the introduction of the government-funded Nursery Education Grant, enabled for the first time, all parents/carers of pre-school age children to access up to 12 hours of free nurs-ery education. Links to broader policy concerned with reducing poverty, greater social inclusion and increased opportunities for children to be cared for, meant that there were greater possibilities for parents to join the workforce.

The Labour government demonstrated a continued commitment to improved outcomes for all children, and equality of opportunity. This has been evident in contemporary and ever-changing policy: (Every Child Matters 2004; Children Act 2005; Childcare Act 2006; The Children's Plan 2007; The Curriculum Guidance for the Foundation Stage (2000) and The Early Years Foundation Stage Framework (EYFS) (2008).

A key element of the NCS was its emphasis on linking care and education to encourage a more holistic view of the needs and development of young children. Prior to the imple-mentation of the EYFS, pedagogical and regulatory approaches to Early Years' practice varied, dependent on the nature of the setting, and there was a distinct view that the PVI sector was the 'poor relation' to the maintained sector. This perception was compounded by the significant difference in status, pay and terms and conditions of service, and the expectations of both curriculum provision, and regulatory standards (Hevey, 2009).

The introduction of the EYFS was intended to provide a framework to reassure parents that, regardless of the type of Early Years provision they chose to use, their child would be kept safe and helped to thrive. The term '**Early Years provider**' is now commonly used to describe any Early Years setting which follows the EYFS. What is significant now is that all providers, regardless of their designation, will have a

> *legal responsibility to comply with the provisions set out in the landmark Childcare Act 2006 ... to ensure that their provision meets the learning and development requirements, and complies with the welfare regulations, as required by Section 40 of the Act.*

> (DfES, 2007, page 8)

The themes and commitments that underpin the DCSF (2008) clearly reflect this and are designed to assist all children in achieving the five outcomes of the Every Child Matters (ECM) agenda. At the same time, the notion of 'joined-up' working has also become a sig-nificant feature of government policy. All stakeholders are expected to share responsibility for the planning and delivery of services for children and their families. Further consider-ation of multi-agency working will be considered in the Children's Centre section of this chapter, and in Chapters 5 and 6.

One final development, which is significant to your work as an Early Years practitioner, is the government's aim to 'professionalise' the Early Years workforce. Findings from the influential Effective Provision of Pre-School Education (EPPE) study (Sylva et al., 2004) found that, where settings employed a trained teacher who acted as manager, and a good proportion of the staff were graduate/teacher qualified, then *effectiveness* for influencing a child's development and progress were improved (Siraj-Blatchford and Manni, 2006). These studies have led to a commitment to a structured career and qualification framework for the Early Years workforce, and the aspiration to have a Graduate Leader (EYP) leading practice in all settings delivering the EYFS by 2015 (CWDC, 2008). However, a highly contentious debate concerned with parity of pay, status and conditions of service between qualified teachers and EYPS practitioners continues to create a divide between the maintained and non-maintained sectors. The perpetuation of low pay within the PVI sector has traditionally undermined efforts to raise the quality of the Early Years workforce. This has been compounded by low minimum qualification requirements and the absence of a clear career ladder. Traditionally, higher qualifications in this sector do not necessarily equate to extra pay, responsibility, or to professional development (Cooke and Lawton, 2008). Only time will tell whether the roles of qualified teacher and EYP will ever be regarded as worthy of equal pay and status. Dependent on the programme of study you have chosen – and your future career aspiration – this is an issue you will need to be sensitive about while on placement. Fundamentally, whatever graduate status you eventually receive, you will still be expected to provide high quality provision for all children in your care.

> ### PRACTICAL TASK
>
> Locate a copy of the Every Child Matters Outcomes Framework. *Identify which particular outcomes you think are pertinent to the work of practitioners in your setting.*
>
> *Interview staff in your placement setting to gather their views.*

The private, voluntary and independent sector

The independent and private sector

The growth of the feminist movement in the 1970s led to an increase in the number of mothers taking up paid employment during their children's earliest years. It became apparent that, due to the lack of state funding for day care provision, there was a gap in the market. This quickly became filled by independent nurseries, which were, in the main, run as profit-making businesses (Fitzgerald and Kay, 2008). Consequently, this sector of childcare provision has traditionally been used by working and professional families who are able to afford to pay fees. The range of provision available in the private sector alone is vast. You may find yourself placed in a small private 'nursery school', which provides sessional care and education for children between the ages of two and five, usually during term time only. At the other end of the spectrum, you may be placed in a private day nursery, providing day care for children as young as three months to school starting age. Private day nurseries offer extended opening times to meet the needs of working families and may remain open up to 11 hours (for example, 7 a.m.– 6 p.m.). Indeed, the decline of the extended family, and increase in number of parents working shift patterns, has recently resulted in some growth in demand for nurseries to provide overnight care. Some large day nurseries can accommodate up to 100 (or even more) children in any one setting, and a large number of 'nursery chains' operate on this scale. Such settings often exhibit a corporate brand through aspects such as policy, uniform and interior design – regardless of geographic location.

This element of the sector has at times received bad press, with terms such as 'baby farming' used to describe groups of children of the same age cared for collectively. It is important that you are aware of this tension, but do not accept this criticism at face value. Standards of quality and care across the whole childcare sector can be variable – which is why there is a very specific regulatory system provided by OFSTED. Clearly, the larger the organisation, the more challenging it may be to ensure provision is sufficiently personalised and quality assured. Nevertheless, the rationale for the establishment of day care provision is not always concerned with making a large profit. Many founders of day nurseries, including large corporate chains, established their business with a clear rationale, the identification of a gap in a particular market, and a desire to provide high quality provision which meets the needs of families.

The organisation of a private nursery will be unique to each setting. One of the key challenges for this sector is to provide appropriate accommodation for young children. Regulation necessitates systems and routines be established to ensure consistent and appropriate care. Yet, this in turn, can sometimes lead to more 'institutionalised' care, which is a far cry from the natural, intimate care a child will receive in their home environment.

It is vitally important that you are aware of the needs of young children who are cared for in a day care environment. There has been significant interest and debate regarding the long-term impact on young children's social, emotional and cognitive development when they spend extended periods of time in day care settings. Recent research concerned with **secure attachment** and **key person** has significantly influenced the development of effective practice, particularly in the day care sector. These issues will be explored more explicitly in Chapter 5.

Many day nursery settings are organised to accommodate children in age-specific rooms. Terms such as 'baby room', 'toddler room' or 'Tweenies' are synonymous with this sector. It is important that the physical layout of the room reflects the needs of the children. Key points of transition, when children 'move up' to the next room, must also be managed sensitively and appropriately. This will be explored in more detail in Chapter 6.

CHALLENGES and DILEMMAS

One of the key challenges for a manager or owner of a day nursery is the implementation of the EYFS Welfare requirements which take account of the organisation of staff to ensure that all staff are allocated appropriate working patterns, including rest breaks. You may find during your placement that there is a range of staff who work in any one room to allow for staff to take rest breaks, plan future activities and to ensure that there are sufficient staff to cover the whole day of care from 7 a.m.– 6 p.m.

continued

CHALLENGES and DILEMMAS *continued*

What do you think are the challenges for a day care setting in ensuring that these elements of effective practice are in place, while at the same time ensuring they also sub-scribe to welfare requirements? Discuss your answer with other students on your course.

The voluntary sector

The development of provision within the voluntary sector gained momentum during the 1950s and early 60s with the establishment of the Playgroups Association in 1962. This group was formed at a key time when there was an increased concern by parents about the lack of nursery education for children. The association (later renamed as the Pre-School Learning Alliance – PLA) was founded by Belle Tutaev, and a key challenge for the group was to lobby for pre-school education and support the development of community-based playgroups (Baldock et al., 2005). Due to the community-based nature of the playgroup, many groups were established within community-based buildings. These ranged from community centres to church and village halls. Playgroups relied heavily on voluntary staff, and on mothers, to provide play-based activities and experiences for children, within the two to five age range. As the buildings were usually used by other community members as well, many playgroups did not have the luxury of operating within a purpose-built envi-ronment. It was (and still is) not uncommon for furniture and resources to be stored away in a cupboard, and set up at the beginning of a session every day. Many playgroups ran on a 'not-for-profit basis'. Session fees would be charged to pay for room hire, resources and some staff salaries. As you can imagine, the sustainability of any playgroup was heav-ily reliant on a regular payment of fees, and the offer of voluntary help by willing parents and community members.

The term playgroup became **pre-school** in 1995, but the way in which they are run still remains the same. This arm of the Early Years sector has undergone the most noteworthy of change since the inception of the NCS. Other than statutory inspections to ensure safe prac-tice and provision under the Children Act (1948 and later 1989), there was, previously, little other statutory guidance or regulation to guide practice, including any requirement for staff to have childcare qualifications. The most influential body supporting practice and advocat-ing pre-school provision was the Pre-school Learning Alliance (PLA). Many pre-schools were, and still are, affiliated to this organisation. It remains the key organisation helping to shape and influence policy, and is the voice of this, sometimes undervalued, sector.

It is important to recognise that not all pre-schools are linked to the PLA. There are a number of charities, such as Barnados and NCH, who also fund and support community-based pre-school provision.

Changes to funding and EYFS Statutory requirements have changed the face of the tra-ditional pre-school. Government targets laying out intentions to have a graduate leader in every Early Years setting, recognised qualifications for all staff, and very clear guidance regarding practice, have all meant that in order for many pre-schools to successfully main-tain their rightful place within the sector, they have had to make significant changes to their practice. It is important that you have an understanding of some of these issues. Regardless of whether you are a teacher working in a nursery class, paid according to teachers' pay and terms and conditions, or a pre-school assistant paid slightly above minimum wage for only the hours you work with children in the setting, you will be required to plan for, provide and support children's learning experiences, make effective assessments which are carefully documented and be accountable to OFSTED and to parents. Many practitioners working in the pre-school sector may not necessarily have entered the childcare profession for the same reasons as someone who wishes to gain graduate status and take a leadership role, but they have a passion and desire to work with children, and are committed to the principles connected to the historical heritage of the pre-school movement. It is vitally important that you understand and respect all colleagues that you work with, and are aware of the tensions and issues that are apparent within this sector.

CHALLENGES and DILEMMAS

- *The outdoor area is located at the back of the church hall, through two additional doors. Children have to be supervised in order to get to the area. How do you provide for safe and flexible 'free flow' outdoor play?*
- *There is no access to running water within the room the pre-school operates. How could you best provide opportunities for messy and water play?*
- *The pre-school is situated in a community centre. The room is also used by Brownies and the local youth club. There is a tendency for any displays of children's learning to be damaged due to the regular use of the room by other users. How else could you display children's work so that you are celebrating their achievements and communicating with parents?*

Children's Centres and Family Centres

Children's Centres evolved from the Sure Start initiative, which was established by New Labour in 1998. This initiative reflected the government's thinking concerned with prevention and early intervention through 'joined-up working'. The initiative developed initially into the Sure Start Local Programmes (SSLP), where the programmes operated in the 10 per cent most deprived electoral wards in the county. The intention of the programme was to work with parents and their children until their fourth birthday. Services on offer included family support, health, education and childcare.

Frost and Parton (2009) discuss the way this exemplified the government's idea of joined-up working, and refer to the official summary of SSLPs.

Sure Start local programmes form a cornerstone of the Government's drive to tackle child poverty and social exclusion, based on firm evidence of what works. They are concentrated in neighbourhoods where a high proportion of children are living in poverty and where Sure Start local programmes can help them to succeed by pioneering new ways of working to improve services.

(Sure Start Unit, 1998, page 37)

They go on to refer to the key period of the development of SSLPs during 1999–2006 as representing a *vibrant area of child welfare development*, where *Local programmes were exciting, innovative, embedded in local communities, often employing local people and spawning numerous narratives of change for parents, children and staff* (Frost and Parton, 2009, page 118). The government was keen to capture the apparent success of the initiative (although see the National Evaluation of Sure Start [Belkey et al., 2007] to explore some of the tensions and issues). There was a growing concern regarding the inequalities for those families who, although would have benefited from the services offered within the SSLP, were unable to access them as they lived in neighbouring 'non-SSLP' areas. The well-known debate concerning 'postcode lottery' led to the next stage of the government's commitment to nationwide 'joined-up' working. It was announced by the government in 2003 that by 2010 there would be a network 3,500 Children's Centres across the nation, which would carry the legacy of the SSLP (Sure Start Unit, 2003).

The aim of the Children's Centre is to enable children and families in every community to receive a 'core offer' of services. In the most deprived 30 per cent local areas this includes:

• integrated early learning and childcare;

• family support – including support and advice on parenting, information about services available in the area and access to specialist, targeted services;

• child and family health services, including antenatal and post-natal support; advice on health and nutrition and speech and language therapy;

• links with Job Centre Plus to encourage and support parents and carers who wish to consider training and employment;

• quick and easy access and referral to wider services.

(DfES, 2007)

If you are placed in a Children's Centre, then you may well be aware that each centre is unique in its physical design and distribution of services. The programme of development of the Children's Centres followed three phases. In the first phase, Children's Centres were developed in areas that served the 20 per cent most disadvantaged wards. Many of these centres were purpose built and all services located in one building. Phase two centres were aimed at families living in the 30 per cent next most disadvantaged wards, and the final phase is concerned with ensuring there is a Children's Centre in every community by 2010. A phase three centre will most probably look very different to the earlier centres. Although there is still a requirement that the core offer of services is available to families, it is worth noting that the services reflect the economic and social needs of a community – there is no longer a need for one single building which provides a 'one stop shop' for families. For example, a phase three centre may only consist of an administrative base for a range of professionals – with the work they do based on an outreach model. Alternatively, purpose-built buildings (such as a health centre) may already provide many elements of the core offer. The statutory childcare element of the offer is not applicable in phase three centres, but there is a requirement that there is sufficient childcare available within a community to meet its needs (see Childcare Act 2006).

Many Children's Centres began their lives in other forms. LAs chose to utilise buildings and services that already existed, and adapted and extended them in order to provide the core offer. A large number of Children's Centres are based on a school site. Maintained Nursery schools and classes have been transformed into Children's Centres through additional building work in order to provide the day care element of the offer and the family and health services which are required. Other centres may be located on sites that are already providing services from another discipline. These include adaptations to health centres, and some Family Centres.

It is important that you do not confuse the purpose of a Family Centre with a Children's Centre. Family Centres are generally sited in areas that are accessible to the most vulnerable families. The services can be provided by either the statutory or voluntary sector, and the main focus of the work with families may vary, depending on their origins. Professionals work with families by assessing their needs and providing support to develop and maintain positive family relationships. Many Family Centres also provide a day care element to their provision, which provides opportunities for young children to attend nursery. Families are not required to pay fees for nursery places, as the provision is specifically targeted at those children who are deemed at risk, and are specifically referred to the nursery by the professionals who support them. The work that takes place within a Family Centre is focused upon early intervention and prevention. Family Centres have a long established history of working in a multidisciplinary context and the work can be clearly evidenced as a forerunner to the ECM agenda. Hanson and Rutledge (2005) provide an insightful report which outlines the role of Family Centres in encouraging learning and understanding with families. It captures the significant impact such work can have not only on individual parents, but for families and the wider community.

It could be contested that whereas Family Centres provide targeted services and support for the most vulnerable families, Children's Centres (especially those in the 'phase three' localities) provide a universal range of services for all families. It is worth taking account of how LAs chose to view Family Centres once the Children's Centre initiative gained momentum. Some LAs have chosen to maintain the unique identity and work of Family Centres – keeping their function and role pertinent and separate for the most vulnerable of families. Others have chosen to combine the work of both centres (commonly naming them as Children and Family Centres). A sound argument can be made for the relevant merits of both options, but there is one key contention concerned with the voice of the most vulnerable child and family. In an ideal world, communities are accepting of diversity and need – but the reality for many families is that they are subject to stigma and prejudice. Successful multi-professional/disciplinary working is still an ideal that is fraught with challenges. Many professionals are understandably attached to their own professional heritage, and the ways of working which accord to that heritage. Frost and Parton (2009, page 180), for example discuss the paradox of a social worker having a *strong sense of professional identity*, with a commitment to *its specific values and techniques*, while at the same time much of their work being focused on *developing integrated working and a shared sense of identity with other professionals*. Taking that into account, it is important that services do not lose sight of the sensitivities involved in working with vulnerable families at the expense of normalising the experience for all.

While on placement, you may well become aware of some of the challenges of working in a multidisciplinary context. Some of those challenges may have been more evident in the early days of the establishment of a centre. Nevertheless, as the team becomes established, and with the effective leadership of the Centre Manager, the benefits should far outweigh the disadvantages. If you are placed within a Children's Centre, then try to utilise the opportunity to see how your work as an Early Years practitioner contributes to the holistic care, learning and development of young children.

PRACTICAL TASK

While on placement, take the opportunity to become involved in other aspects of the centre, in addition to the day care element. What benefits can you see to working in this context in relation to ECM?

The maintained sector: the education context

The 1944 Education Act required that children start school the term after their fifth birthday. For many young children, the reality was that they actually started school up to twelve months earlier than this. There have been a number of factors that have contributed to this, but in the main they are government policy and society's infatuation with 'school readiness'.

The Plowden Report (DES, 1967) advocated the need for high quality Early Years provision on a part-time basis for all children over the age of three whose parents wanted it. This led to the development of the traditional nursery school, or class, which was intended as the precursor to the Reception year. A significant feature of a nursery school or class has been the requirement for a qualified teacher to lead practice with the support of a well-qualified assistant – traditionally known as a Nursery Nurse holding the National Nursery Nurse Examining Body (NNEB) qualification. Ratios of adult to child within the maintained sector are generally higher than those in the PVI sector (as discussed earlier). It is not unusual to see up to one adult to every 13 children. You may have noted from your experience that the ratios are far lower in the PVI sector (1:8 for children three years and above). The welfare requirements of the EYFS continue to reflect this disparity. The argument for the different staffing requirements between the two sectors has been substantiated by the research findings of the EPPE Report (Sylva et al., 2004), which articulates that children's achievements both socially and cognitively are greater in settings that are led by qualified teachers. This is an interesting debate when we consider factors related to key person and attachment. Although many qualified teachers may well be of the mind that their experience and qualifications may have some benefit to the experiences they provide for children, conversely, they may well argue that given the choice, they would be much more confident in providing key emotional support for children if they were responsible for eight rather than thirteen children!

The further influence that has impacted on the maintained sector was the introduction of the National Curriculum in 1988. This policy saw the introduction of SATs for children at the end of Key Stage 1. Although the policy did not directly relate to children under the age of five, there has been some significant argument that Key Stage 1 teachers felt pressure for children to achieve well in their SATs. This in turn led to a more formalised approach to learning within the Early Years (see Cox and Sanders, 1994, for example). Over the following years, Early Years teachers have worked with three different Curriculum frameworks (*Desirable Learning Outcomes* (1996); *Curriculum Guidance for the Foundation Stage* (2000) and *The Early Years Foundation Stage* (2008)) – each one progressively focusing on less formal learning, and more experiential learning as the basic pedagogical approach. During this period of time, in 2002, the Foundation Stage was formally established as part of the National Curriculum, and the early years of a child's life were at last recognised as a unique and significant stage. The principles underpinning the frameworks clearly stated the importance of an experiential, play-based approach to learning, rather than a prescribed curriculum.

Nevertheless, the pressures concerned with readiness for testing have not disappeared, and continue to be present as children start full-time schooling in their Reception year. This is outlined by recent research (Adams et al., 2004). The interpretation of the EYFS requirement, and how this is translated into practice, is heavily dependent on the beliefs and values regarding young children's learning by the head and senior managers of the school (Keating et al., 2002). This may also be translated into how children are organised within the EYFS. A traditional model of Early Years provision within a school context may be to accommodate nursery and Reception aged children separately. The nursery age children will be offered up to 15 hours of 'nursery education' each week. Schools are required to provide a range of offers from which parents can select those that best suit their own circumstances. Options may include a traditional three-hour 'morning' or 'afternoon' session, or combinations of whole and half days.

Some schools have found opportunities to accommodate all children within the EYFS age phase together. To the untrained eye this can feel very much like organised chaos, with children going home for lunch, and others joining the class at 1 p.m. for their afternoon session. Teachers have to provide routines and an appropriate environment that take account of the needs of nursery age children attending sessional care, alongside Reception children who are attending school for the whole day.

Small schools have less flexibility in how they organise their classes. It is not uncommon to see Reception children taught alongside Key Stage 1 aged children. This is a significant challenge for teachers who are required to not only organise, plan and deliver learning experiences based on two different pedagogical frameworks (EYFS and National Curriculum), but are also mindful of the differences in maturity and experience which impact on how children respond to learning experiences. One key aspect for all teachers within the school context is concerned with supporting children in the transition from Reception to Key Stage 1. Research by Sanders et al. (2005) highlights the challenges of moving from a play-based curriculum to more structure; difficulties with less mature children in coping with the transition and parental concerns. These are very real challenges for teachers to deal with. Issues concerned with transition are considered in the Wider Context commitment in 'Enabling Environments' and will be considered further in Chapter 6 of this book.

During the time of writing this book, a general election has taken place. After thirteen years of Labour administration, the party failed to be re-elected for a fourth time. The country is now led by a coalition government between the Conservative and Liberal Democratic parties. This is also a time of immense economic hardship. There is no doubt that changes to government policy will reflect the necessity to reduce public spending. As you read this chapter in particular, it is important that you are mindful of the impact on Early Years services and provision that any changes to government policy may have.

C H A P T E R   S U M M A R Y

This chapter has provided an overview of the historical and political development of Early Years provision over the last 40 years. It has examined in closer detail some of the unique features of the range of Early Years settings you may encounter during your placements. Finally, you should now have an understanding of some of the issues and challenges that are pertinent to individual Early Years providers, with a consideration of the implications for your own personal and professional development.

REFERENCES

Adams, S, Alexander, E, Drummond, M and Moyles, J (2004) *Inside the Foundation Stage – Recreating the Reception Year. Final Report.* London: ATL Publications.

Baldock, P (2001) *Regulating Early Years Services.* London: David Fulton.

Baldock, P, Fitzgerald, D and Kay, J (2005) *Understanding Early Years Policy.* London: Paul Chapman.

Belsky, J, Barnes, J and Melhuish, E (2007) *The National Evaluation of Sure Start.* Bristol: Policy Press.

Bowlby, J (1958) The Nature of a Child's Tie to His Mother. *International Journal of Psychoanalysis,* 4: 89–113.

Children's Workforce Development Council (CWDC) (2008) *Clear Progression 2008: The Next Steps Towards Building an Integrated Qualifications Framework for the Children and Young People's Workforce.* Leeds: CWDC.

Cooke, G and Lawton, K (2008) *For Love or Money: Pay, Progression and Professionalisation in the 'Early Years' Workforce.* London: Institute for Public Policy Research.

Cox, T and Sanders, S (1994) *The Impact on the National Curriculum on the Teaching of Five Year Olds.* London: Falmer Press.

DCSF (2007) *The Children's Plan: Building Better Futures.* London: Stationery Office.

DCSF (2008) *Statutory Framework for the Early Years Foundation Stage.* London: DCSF.

DES (1967) Plowden Report.

DfEE (1998) *Meeting The Childcare Challenge.* London: HMSO.

DfES (1991) *Starting with Quality.* (Rumbold Report). London: HMSO.

DfEE (2000) *Curriculum Guidance for the Foundation Stage.* London: QCA.

DfES (2004) *Every Child Matters: Change for Children.* London: DfES.

DfES (2006) *Childcare Act 2006.* London: HMSO.

DfES (2007) *Governance Guidance for Sure Start Children's Centres and Extended Schools.* London: DfES.

Fitzgerald, D and Kay, J (2008) *Working Together in Children's Services.* London: Routledge.

Frost, N and Parton, N (2009*) Understanding Children's Social Care. Politics, Policy and Practice.* London: Sage.

Hanson, S and Rutledge, H (2005) *Including Families in the Learning Community: Family Centres and the Expansion of Learning.* York: Joseph Rowntree Foundation.

Hevey, D (2009) Professional Work in Early Childhood, in Waller. T, *An Introduction to Early Childhood* (2nd ed). London: Sage.

Sanders, D. Whitre, G, Burge, B, Sharp, C, Eames, A, McEune, R and Grayson, H (2005) *A Study of Transition from the Foundation Stage to Key Stage 1.* London: SureStart.

SCAA (1996) *Nursery Education: Desirable Outcomes for Children's Learning on Entering Compulsory Schooling.* London: DfEE.

Siraj-Blatchford, I and Manni, L (2006) *Effective Leadership in the Early Years Sector (ELEYS) Study.* Institute of Education, University of London.

Sure Start Unit (1998) *Guide for Sure Start Trailblazers.* London: DfES.

Sylva, K, Melhuish, EC, Sammons, P, Siraj-Blatchford, I and Taggart, B (2004) *The Final Report: Effective Pre-School Education.* London: DfES/Institute of Education, University of London.

FURTHER READING

Cooke, G and Lawton, K (2008) *For Love or Money: Pay, Progression and Professionalisation in the 'Early Years' Workforce.* London: Institute for Public Policy Research.

Hevey, D (2009) Professional Work in Early Childhood, in Waller. T, *An Introduction to Early Childhood* (2nd ed). London: Sage.

Sanders, D. Whitre, G, Burge, B, Sharp, C, Eames, A, McEune, R and Grayson, H (2005) *A Study of Transition from the Foundation Stage to Key Stage 1.* London: SureStart.

Siraj-Blatchford, I and Manni, L (2006) *Effective Leadership in the Early Years Sector (ELEYS) Study.* Institute of Education, University of London.

2 Preparing for your placement

Carolyn Davis

CHAPTER OBJECTIVES

By the end of this chapter you should:

- *understand why placements are valuable and vital to your professional development;*
- *have begun to understand what it means to be a reflective practitioner and have begun to develop skills of reflection which will support your learning during your placement;*
- *understand what it means to be professional in a placement;*
- *have a developing understanding of the roles, responsibilities and expectations which you are likely to encounter, as part of your placement experience.*

This chapter addresses the following Professional Standards for QTS and EYPS:
QTS: Q2; 3(a) (b); 5; 6; 7(a) (b); 8; 9.
EYPS: S3; 4; 6; 20; 29; 31.

Introduction

This chapter offers you guidance and practical suggestions to support you as you prepare for your placement. It will also give you an opportunity to consider the professional roles and responsibilities you may be expected to take on. Some aspects of preparing for a placement, such as making sure you understand the requirements of your course and what is expected of you as you move through your time in a professional setting, are likely to be similar for everyone. Some features will be different though and these will depend on your training route and the type of placement setting.

Whatever your final qualification or outcome will be, and whatever setting you are offered for placement (see Chapter 1 for an idea of the range and diversity of Early Years settings), the most important thing will be your own readiness to engage with the learning opportunities offered. Leeson (2004, page 154) says that placements contribute to trainees' development into *rounded individuals* and *thoughtful engaged practitioners*.

In essence, a placement enables you to experience a professional work situation but actually offers you so much more than just work experience. You should have the chance to:

- engage in reflective practice – to think about what you do and say, how you behave and respond, and to honestly reflect on how this affects others, whether lessons can be learned and whether changes need to be made;

- enrich your academic study by integrating and making links between your placement experiences and study – linking theory and practice;

- develop professionally and get to know your professional self more.

So let's take each of the above and look at them in more detail.

Becoming a reflective practitioner

Reflective practice, or the importance of thinking over actions past and present and identifying the lessons learnt for future action, should be a crucial aspect of professional work and lifelong learning.

(Leeson, 2004, page 233)

This statement emphasises the importance of developing the ability to mull over your day-to-day experiences, consider why things happened the way they did and think about what might need to be changed in the light of what you have learned. This is about becoming a reflective, analytical practitioner who can find ways of standing back and looking with more objective eyes.

One way of thinking about this is to try to make the familiar *unfamiliar*, to try to see things with new eyes.

REFLECTIVE TASK

Think about something which you do routinely, day-after-day, which you don't think much about any more. Consider an everyday practical task that needs to be done at home such as washing-up, ironing or vacuuming. Choose one and allow yourself to stand back, creating some distance between yourself and the task.

You need now to try to see the task through the eyes of another. Maybe you could imagine that you meet someone with no experience of what you are doing or why you are doing it. Try to explain by asking yourself some key questions:

- *Why are you doing the task?*
- *Who are you doing it for?*
- *What is the point of doing it?*
- *What do you want to achieve at the end of the task?*

As you are thinking, make some brief notes of the answers and anything else that comes to mind as you reflect.

Now consider a professional duty that has become part of your custom and practice – reading a story at the end of the day, for example – ideally something which is done as a matter of course and maybe something which you haven't thought about much before. Can you use the same technique to reflect on this element of your professional practice?

What conclusions do you come to? What has surprised you about where your thinking has led you? What could or would you change in the future? Why and how?

Your placement will be the ideal time to develop the confidence to be self-evaluative and come to your own conclusions. You will have the chance to find what Featherstone, Munby and Russell (1997, page 1) call a *professional voice*, to begin to develop professional authority and a professional point of view. They agree with Richert's assertion that: *Such knowledge empowers the individual by providing a source for action that is generated from within rather than imposed from without* ... (1997, page 1).

Most courses require the placement setting to make sure you have a mentor or supervisor to guide your thinking and support your professional development. They should try to make sure you have time in a busy week to reflect on what you have been doing, mull things over and think about how you can learn from your experiences. This will depend on the nature of your course and the amount of time you are expected to be in contact with children.

Murray (2006, page 67) asserts that, *Successful mentoring recognises its potential value by enabling the practitioner to make the most of the rich experiential learning resource which is the workplace.* The point here is that, alongside a more experienced professional who can offer you support, encouragement and assistance, your placement experience will provide opportunities for initiation into professional relationships, proficiencies, events and routines through professional reflection. In other words, you will be able to work in collaboration with your mentor, and develop the necessary knowledge and understanding, both formal and more informal, that you will need to acquire and assimilate into your professional development. For Street (2004), these relationships between a learner and a mentor are, *at their heart, teaching and learning relationships in which the participants are cognitively and affectively changed by their participation.* Your relationship and contact with your mentor is likely to be pivotal to your learning and development and will help you to move, both literally and metaphorically, towards your goals.

But who are these people and what are *their* roles and responsibilities? Do you understand the expectations in terms of *your* responsibilities and if not, where will you access this information? Who could you discuss this with so that you feel prepared for relationships that will be a crucial part of your professional development?

Here are some of the names typically associated with the mentor role. This is not an exhaustive list and you may be able to add some yourself.

- Mentor.
- Placement or Setting Mentor.
- Placement Tutor.
- Link Assessment Tutor.
- Advisor.
- Visiting Tutor.
- Coach.
- Supervisor.

When preparing for your placement experience it is worth spending some time defining the roles of the different people who may act in a 'mentoring' capacity. For this you will need to:

● establish a clear definition of their role;

● consider mutual expectations of the relationship.

Your course requirements will also probably necessitate you to undertake some more formal tasks during your placement as well as encouraging you to consider everything you do from day to day.

Examples of more formal reflective tasks could be:

● making observations of children engaged in particular activities;

● observing other staff interacting with children;

● planning activities for individuals and groups and thinking about how children respond;

● reflecting critically on professional reading and considering how this might impact on or refresh your practice;

● undertaking a reflective journal where you document key experiences and show how you have engaged with the issues raised for you, providing your own critique;

● gathering information to inform an assignment on a particular issue.

On a day-to-day basis you will also need to ponder on:

● the activities you undertake with children, whether planned by you or by others;

● how you monitor and record children's development – and what you do with what you find out!

● the nature of your relationships with children and the quality of your interactions with them;

● how you engage and communicate with other staff and parents;

● how you develop a rich, purposeful and safe learning environment;

● how you understand and deal with issues of diversity and inclusion – ethnicity, disability, gender, class, religion, and sexuality.

There are many different ways to engage in reflection but the key is a willingness to change and the ability to maintain an open-minded approach to your thinking. Essentially, you are going to do research and to do this effectively you need to try to develop a research mindset, that is:

> *...an orientation towards continuing learning, a belief that every opportunity brings with it fresh opportunities for learning something new or understanding something differently.*

> (Willan, 2004, page 171)

REFLECTIVE TASK

Consider something that you have already learnt to do such as driving a car, playing a musical instrument or playing a game. Think about how you were able to learn, what you needed to do, whether anyone helped you and how.

Use the following stages based on those identified by Herbert and Rothwell (2005, page 46) to help you think about the process you went through.

- *Wanting – why did you want to learn? What motivated you and made you enthusiastic?*
- *Planning – how long did it take for you to learn the skill, who helped you and how did you find out what to do?*
- *Action – what activities did you do to help you learn?*
- *Feedback – how did you know how you were doing? Did you ask/need anyone else to evaluate your progress?*
- *Reflection – were you successful? Have you finished learning the skill or do you need to do more? Is there anything you could have done better?*
- *Thinking – what next? What do you need to do to improve?*

PRACTICAL TASK

Find out about the professional standards that you will be expected to achieve by the end of your training. You will find these in your course information or you can research them on the internet. Read the standards carefully, thinking about what they may involve. Use them to identify your strengths, that is, attributes you already possess or skills and knowledge you have already achieved.

Now think about what you would like to get from your placement. Think about where you are now and what you need to develop. What are your professional development needs? It might help to think in terms of effective practice, knowledge and understanding, your professional attitudes and mindset and interpersonal and communication skills. Write yourself a short action plan asking yourself the following questions:

- *What do you want to learn and why (your initial targets)?*
- *Who will help you and how will you find out what to do?*
- *What professional activities will you need to undertake to help you learn?*
- *How will you know whether you are making progress and who will help you to measure how you are doing?*
- *If you are successful how will you know?*
- *What will you need to do next to further your learning?*
- *What would your subsequent target(s) be?*

Linking theory and practice

It will be important not to see the two aspects of theory and practice as separate and opposing forces in competition with one another but more as complementary facets, which enhance your experience as you achieve a balance and harmonisation between them. You will probably enter a placement setting with knowledge acquired from taught sessions, independent study and previous practical experience. You will need to be prepared to be challenged by new experiences, assimilate them into previous study, creating new links and associations which can then become the basis of the development of practice and further learning.

The *Every Child Matters* document (2004, pages 16–17) identified five outcomes for children:

- Being healthy.

- Staying safe.

- Enjoying and achieving.

- Making a positive contribution.

- Economic well-being.

These outcomes are reflected in the four themes of the *Statutory Framework for the Early Years Foundation Stage: Setting the Standards for Learning, Development and Care for Children from Birth to Five* (DfES, 2007), which is designed to ensure continuity of care and planning for children's development across the variety of different Early Years providers from which parents can choose.

As professionals working with the youngest children we must aim to nurture:

- A Unique Child, supporting every child into becoming a *competent learner from birth who can be resilient, capable, confident and self-assured.*

- Positive Relationships, within which children *learn to be strong and independent from a base of loving and secure relationships with parents and/or a key person.*

- Enabling Environments, which play a *key role in supporting and extending children's development and learning.*

- Learning and Development – children develop and learn in different ways and at different rates and all areas of Learning and Development are equally important and inter-connected.

(DfES, 2007, pages 08–09)

All settings must, by law, use the EYFS document and the idea is that a child will experience high quality provision in whatever setting they spend their pre-school years. The emphasis is on a holistic view of development and means that the ability to link theory and practice is vital to the well-being of the children in your care. Children will only spend time in your setting once. This means that every practitioner in every setting has responsibility to ensure better quality outcomes for children and to be the best practitioner possible.

CASE STUDY

Joanne was due to begin a placement in a setting where many different home languages were spoken by the children. She knew she would encounter children who had very little experience of speaking English. Discussion with the setting manager revealed that 50 per cent of the children spoke Urdu or Punjabi at home; around 20 per cent had a Bangladeshi heritage and there were growing communities of Somali and Rumanian families around the setting, some of whom would make up the other 30 per cent of children. Joanne knew that her experience of supporting children with English as an additional language (EAL) was limited to a college session and the background reading she had done. In a previous placement all the children had spoken English as a first language.

Joanne made a list of the things she needed to do as she prepared for the placement:

1 *Re-read college notes about supporting children with EAL*

2 *Go to the library*

3 *Research on the internet*

4 *Think about how I can link my reading and thinking with real life practice*

5 *Talk to the manager about spending some time observing other professionals in the setting*

6 *Make notes about how practitioners support children with EAL*

7 *Reflect on what knowledge, understanding and skills I will need to develop*

8 *Talk to my mentor about how I can personalise learning and development for individual children*

9 *Start to think about my professional targets and talk to my mentor and the setting manager about how I can achieve these.*

Think about what motivated you to want to work with children and their families. However you came to the decision, many people express their motivation as 'wanting to make a difference'. Your professional skills, knowledge and understanding, ways of engaging with others and the attitudes you adopt will affect those you work with. Your placement will be an opportunity to reflect on the relationship between the theoretical knowledge you may have learned through college sessions, your own study and the everyday professional routines and procedures you observe and experience. You will have the chance to combine theory and practice and investigate the links between the two.

…being a professional is more than simply meeting a set of external criteria. The capacity continually to ask oneself what it really means to be a professional within the Early Years, to continue enquiring about why you do things the way you do in your practice and to probe your beliefs and philosophy of childhood is of fundamental importance.

(Wild and Mitchell, 2007, page XV)

Getting to know your professional self

Your placement will give you the opportunity to experience being a member of staff and to explore the roles and responsibilities of a practitioner in that particular type of setting. Before we move on to an exploration of the role of your placement in developing your professional self and the role of your placement workplace as a learning community, there are some basic professional behaviours you will need to take into consideration.

Confidentiality

During your placement you will be professionally involved with children, their families and other staff. You will, therefore, be expected to maintain an appropriate level of confidentiality. Think about the possible consequences of gossiping in a negative way about one member of staff to another or to a parent about a child who is not theirs.

> **PRACTICAL TASK**
>
> *Find out about any relevant policies or particular issues regarding confidentiality before you begin your placement.*

Child protection and 'safeguarding'

If you encounter issues of child protection, these will need very careful consideration and handling.

> **PRACTICAL TASK**
>
> *Find out, as part of your placement preparation, who is the named person for Child Protection and what procedure you would be expected to follow if you are worried about a child. Never talk about your worries or a disclosure of experience of abuse to anyone who does not need to know. Make sure you have read and understand the setting's policy regarding child protection. This will help protect you in your relationships with children as well as making sure that you know what to do in difficult situations.*

Making sure that children are safe is a legal requirement and will constitute an immensely important part of your training and your future work with children and families. Chapter 4 will offer you more information on 'safeguarding' children but if you want to find out more at this stage look at the 'Suggested learning outcomes for target groups'. See also Chapter 4 of *Working Together to Safeguard Children* (HM Government, 2006) which is available from:

www.everychildmatters.gov.uk/socialcare/safeguarding.

This information is for practitioners, those who supervise practitioners and volunteers, and those who have strategic responsibility for providing services to children and young people. A clear emphasis is placed on the importance of working together to safeguard children.

Sensitivity

During your placement you will be involved with children in an environment for whom someone else is ultimately responsible. It is possible that you may find that you want to question practice or suggest other ways of doing things. Depending on your placement situation, you may need to act with extra care and sensitivity. Before you begin your placement, make sure that you know whom you can talk to if you need to or ask your mentor or supervisor for advice.

CHALLENGES and DILEMMAS

Imagine that you are a couple of weeks into your placement and you become aware that a member of staff is becoming more and more frustrated with a child who lashes out at other children a number of times a day and snatches toys. The staff member shouts at the child every time this happens and one day grabs the child's arm roughly, pulls her away from the other children saying, 'If you can't play properly, keep away from the other children'.

As part of your preparation for the placement you have already read the Behaviour policy of the setting and feel that the member of staff is not adhering to it and that the child is not being treated and supported as a 'Unique' child.

Think about:

- *How you would feel in this situation?*
- *What do you think you would need to do?*
- *Do you think there is anything you could do to support the child?*
- *What would it be?*
- *Who could you talk to?*
- *What would you say?*

Commitment

Before you begin your placement make sure you know the expectations for beginning and ending your working day and make sure you can get to the setting on time. Find out what other expectations there are and listen to and act upon the advice and suggestions you are offered. Development and demonstration of your commitment and enthusiasm will be an important part of your placement experience.

Feedback and what to expect

During your placement, feedback could be given in a variety of ways and by a variety of different people. Depending on your course and the length of your placement, feedback could be offered by your supervisor, mentor, other staff members, external assessors. You will almost always receive written feedback after observations of your interactions with children and there may be a written report at the end of your placement, and/or regular review statements if your placement is longer than a few weeks in duration. If the setting you are in has a system in place by which the interactions with children, the provision, planning and development of the learning environment is regularly monitored you may find that, as a member of staff for a time, *your* professional performance is monitored too. Quality provision will be expected even if you are not a permanent member of staff.

Verbal feedback may not always happen at specific times set aside for providing support and guidance. You may encounter really valuable information and advice by chatting with other members of staff at the beginning and end of the day and at break times.

Receiving high quality feedback from an experienced and expert other is like having some-one hold up a mirror to your practice, helping you to have glimpses of your professional self as others may perceive you and supporting your learning journey. This will be a vital element of your professional development so it is really important to try to be open to suggestions and recommendations and act upon them where you can. You should expect any feedback that you get to be constructive and supportive and to offer you guidance, advice and recommendations as to how you might improve and develop your practice further. The point of feedback is to help you and others involved with your training to track a path of learning and development as you make progress towards the professional standards expected of you by the end of your training. It should also encourage you to be increasingly reflective about your practice. (See the section 'Becoming a reflective practitioner' earlier in this chapter.)

In order for you to chart your course towards your final goal more effectively you will probably be expected to identify shorter or more long-term targets – stepping stones along the way.

In their book, *Managing Your Placement: A Skills-based Approach,* Herbert and Rothwell discuss the importance of SMART targets (2005, page 74).

SMART stands for targets which are:

• Specific – do your targets say what exactly it is that you need to do?

• Measurable – can you show proof that you have achieved your targets?

• Achievable – are your targets easy enough (but challenging!) to achieve in the time you have been given?

• Realistic – are your targets things that you can really do something about?

• Time-bound – have you decided dates for achieving your targets?

Feedback based on targets that are set after consideration of questions such as those above is more likely to be unambiguous and precise, giving you a clearer indication of how you are doing and what you need to do next to move yourself on in your learning and thinking.

CASE STUDY

Faraz was due to begin a placement with the Pre-school group in a Children's Centre. He was keen to do some thorough preparation in order to get the most from his placement experience and had given a lot of thought to what his initial targets might be. He arranged to visit the setting and talk to the Children's Centre teacher (who had agreed to be his supervisor) about the first couple of weeks of the placement – what he needed to be doing and what he should be aiming to achieve. As Faraz's experience of developing partnerships with parents was limited, they agreed together that developing skills for communicating with and building relationships with parents and carers should be a priority and Faraz suggested the following target:

'To communicate with parents and talk to them about the development of their children'.

Realising that this was an ambiguous and rather 'woolly' target, the supervisor introduced Faraz to the idea of SMART targets. Faraz was encouraged to reflect on his intentions and the steps he needed to take to succeed. Together they agreed on a series of more specific and realistic targets, which Faraz could aim to achieve during his first two weeks in the placement. Then they discussed how Faraz would know that he had reached his goals.

SMART TARGET 1 DATE:	
Specific?	• To take on pastoral responsibility for one child. To observe child regularly over a two-week period and then to meet with parents/carers to discuss child's progress and development.
Measurable?	• Has child been identified? • Have observations been carried out? • Has meeting with parents/carers taken place? • Is there an entry in placement journal focusing how communication skills, knowledge and understanding, attitudes for working with parents/carers have developed? Can you talk about your learning?
Achievable?	• Child will be chosen in discussion with supervisor. • Reasons for observations will be shared with parents/carers and their consent obtained. • Child will be observed regularly. • Observations will be discussed with supervisor. • Meeting with parents/carers will be planned for a fortnight after the beginning of the placement.
Realistic?	• Yes!
Time-bound?	• Week 1 – choose child, share target with parents and arrange meeting. • Weeks 1 and 2 – observe child for at least 15 minutes daily and track for a whole day (Tuesday) in week 2. • Week 2 (Wednesday) – discuss observations with supervisor. • Week 2 (Thursday) – meet with parents. • Week 2 (Friday) – reflect on and write up experience and learning and discuss with supervisor – identify further target(s) if appropriate.

Murray (2006, page 67) describes the workplace as a *rich experiential learning resource*. This is not just about harnessing the broad spectrum of expertise within a placement setting but also providing opportunities for initiation of trainees into professional relationships, events and routines. Do not underestimate the potential of your placement setting to provide a wealth of learning opportunities. In addition to providing you with experience of the actual working practices, involvement with children, parents and staff, and material for assignments or coursework, etc., the others who work with you as colleagues, supervisor, mentor, and so on, will also be fundamental to your learning and development.

Rogoff (1989, page 91), proposes that learning takes place *in situations of joint involvement with more experienced people in culturally important activities*. She terms this process *guided participation* (page 68). Wood (1986, page 91) believes that the most effective instruction is the result of sensitive support and guidance by a more capable partner who provides appropriate (or *contingent*) levels of support during the learning process. He sees this support in terms of *scaffolding*. For him, learning is about knowledge that is *jointly constructed through interaction with those who already embody them* (Wood, 1986, page 102).

REFLECTIVE TASK

Consider the sections dealing with reflective practice and mentoring earlier in this chapter and ask yourself how more experienced others have contributed to your personal and professional development in the past?

Vygotsky believes that all cognitive development has its base in social relations among people. He argues that:

> *All the higher mental functions are interiorised relations of a social order, the basis of the social structure of the personality. Their composition, genetic structure and mode of action, in a word, all of their nature, is social: even when transformed into mental processes it remains quasi-social.*

> (1966, page 41)

In Vygotsky's terms this means that although the important role of someone with more experience cannot be disputed, the learning process is *joint* and the learner and the educator are actively constructing knowledge and understanding *together*.

Lave and Wenger studied the learning of Xerox workers within the context of their organisation. Zimitat (2007) describes how they developed the term *Community of Practice*, referring to a working community of practitioners engaged in the same professional field into which newcomers would enter, become immersed in the culture and begin to acquire the practices of the community. Much has since been written about this powerful idea and how the understanding of the *social mechanisms by which novices are inducted into expert ways of knowing, thinking and reasoning in their professional or practice circle* (Zimitat, 2007) can be more widely applied to professional learning.

Zimitat discusses Lave and Wenger's assertion that people need to physically be together for a Community of Practice to truly develop. It is through actually spending time together, talking and exploring shared issues that you and colleagues, as members of such a *community* during your placement, can begin to solve professional problems, advise and support each other and move individual and collective thinking on. As you progress through your placement, try to recognise the times when your professional community supports learning and development for the members. Examples could be staff meetings, in-service training that you may be involved with, meetings with parents/carers or more informal chats at lunchtimes/break times, etc. Are you able to identify and acknowledge the points at which you experience professional growth because of your involvement with others on your placement? What are your 'light bulb' moments?

Wallace (2006), too declares that:

> The value of community knowledge is that it goes beyond what has been written and unearths the truly difficult-to-know aspects of practice – the nuances, variations, and subtleties that can only be discovered in conversation.

The actual process of beginning to feel like a practitioner, of assuming a professional identity, a process of *assisted becoming* (Edwards, 1988 cited by Hobson et al., 2008, page 424) is how you will be supported into the assimilation of ideas, policies and national frameworks and where this knowledge is absorbed and integrated into your professional practice, contributing to the development of your professional identity.

Your placement should support your induction into professional thought and practice, help to bridge the gap between theory and practice, develop independence and competencies, which contribute to the achievement of the specific requirements of the standards. And because you will spend your time in your placement setting immersed in and engaged in contextualised learning, the time and space is provided for this process of maturity to happen – for you to develop, to get to know and explore your professional self.

And finally ...
'been there and got the t-shirt'

Students who have completed their placements successfully and achieved the professional standards for their course offer some practical advice to you as you prepare for your placement experience.

Be prepared – know your course!

- Have you read and understood the course material, placement booklet, etc?

- Do you know what expectations and professional demands there are of you and of others? Are you expected to do anything outside of normal working hours – parent/practitioner meetings, for example?

- Are you aware of the professional standards for your course?

- Do you know how far you have already progressed towards the standards and do you have an idea of some initial targets that could be set?

- How will you know that you are making progress against the standards and what you still need to do?

- Do you know which standards will be covered during the placement period?

- What are the requirements for evidence of your progress towards the standards?

- Are there any tasks that need to be completed during your placement – logs, journals, projects, reports, etc?

- Are you aware of the guidance on assessment from the beginning of your placement and have you read it carefully so that you have a very clear idea of what you need to aim for?

- Will you be graded at the end of your placement? Do you know what you need to do to achieve the grade you want? How will the grade (if there is one) be verified and by whom?

- Who will be involved in your assessment and how will the process be moderated? Who has the final say?

- Do you know how a 'good' student would be described? Do you know what the criteria would be for receiving a judgement of 'poor' or 'fail'?

- Are you aware of the academic timetable and clear about any important dates for you – placement dates, assignment dates, exam board dates, etc?

- Does anyone else need to know the requirements or expectations for the placement? How will you make sure this is communicated clearly?

- Do you need to set up files for evidence, observations, documenting your experiences and reflections, etc? Are you clear about the guidance? Think about when and how this should be done.

Take responsibility – be proactive!

- Have you made contact with and introduced yourself to the setting? Do they know when you will begin your placement?

- How will you get to know the routines and organisation of the setting?

- How will you make sure you are as involved in the everyday routines, practices and events of the setting as you can be?

- How flexible can you be if adjustments need to be made as things develop?

- Do you need to make domestic arrangements in advance of starting your placement?

- Find out as much as possible about your setting placement, the area and local community and how to get there!

- How will you achieve a balance between your homelife, learning and development needs and the expectations of the setting?

- How can you get the most out of placement preparation visits? If none are planned, can you ask?

- Have you been shown around the setting? If this is not planned, can you ask? Is there a map?

- Do you know:

  - where to find a prospectus?

  - how to get hold of policies, OFSTED reports and any other documents you may need?

  - where to photocopy (if you need to) and find resources?

  - who the first-aider is?

  - who the named person for Child Protection is?

  - the fire-drill?

  - the names and responsibilities of other staff?

  - whether there is a trainee induction pack?

I will survive – getting through if things get tough!

- Remember that apprehension before entering any new situation is natural.

- Day-to-day pressures and stresses are inevitable. How will your reflection time be managed? How will you make sure you have review and feedback time – away from children and other responsibilities? Is this built into your timetable?

- Make sure you know when time is set-aside for you to have contact with your supervisor/mentor. If this is not planned for you – ask!

- Try to build positive relationships with others, beginning before you start your placement.

- Do you know what advice and support is available and how it can be accessed if the expectations of the setting seem unreasonable, if you feel under too much pressure or things don't seem to be working out?

- Do you know when and how your mentor or course tutor can be contacted if you need them?

- Do you have a network of other students, family or friends who can offer support should you need it?

- Is there another student on placement with you; can you share experiences and support one another?

- Make some rules for yourself and try to keep to them. Some examples might be:

  - write things up every night if you can rather than leaving them until the weekend;

  - get enough sleep;

  - take some time for yourself, one night off in the week, for example.

- Remember that there is no such thing as a pointless placement, even if things are not working out as well as you would like. There is always something to learn!

CHAPTER SUMMARY

This chapter has offered guidance supported by relevant theoretical frameworks to help you as you begin to prepare for your placement.

You should have an understanding of:

- the potential of a professional placement to contribute to your professional learning and development;

- the importance of developing skills of reflection and how to prepare to be a reflective practitioner during your placement, including how to begin to set yourself professional targets;

- the role of a 'mentor' in your placement;

- the professional roles and responsibilities that you will need to prepare to take on during your placement.

Finally, a checklist offers you guidance on the very practical things you may need to take into consideration before you begin your placement.

DfES (2004) *Every Child Matters: Change for Children*. London: DfES.

DfES (2007) *Statutory Framework for the Early Years Foundation Stage: Setting the Standards for Learning, Development and Care for Children from Birth to Five*. London: DfES.

Featherstone, D, Munby, H and Russell, T (eds) (1997) *Finding a Voice While Learning to Teach*. London: The Falmer Press.

HM Government (2006) *Working Together to Safeguard Children*. London: HMSO.

Herbert, I and Rothwell, A (2005) *Managing Your Placement: A Skills-based Approach*. Basingstoke: Palgrave Macmillan.

Hobson, A, Malderez, AL, Giannakaki, Pell, G and Tomlinson, PD (2008) Student Teachers' Experiences of Initial Teacher Preparation in England: Core Themes and Variation. *Research Papers in Education*, 23 (4): 407–33.

Leeson, C (2004) In Praise of Reflective Practice, in Willan, J, Parker-Rees, R and Savage, J (eds) *Early Childhood Studies*. Exeter: Learning Matters.

Murray, J (2006) Designing and Implementing a Mentoring Scheme: University of Worcester SureStart-Recognised Sector-endorsed Foundation Degree in Early Years, in Robins, A (ed) *Mentoring in the Early Years*. London: Paul Chapman.

Rogoff, B (1989) The Joint Socialization of Development by Young Children and Adults, in Light, P, Sheldon, S and Woodhead, M (eds) (1991) *Learning to Think*. London: Routledge.

Street, C (2004) Examining Learning to Teach through a Social Lens: How Mentors Guide Newcomers into a Professional Community of Learners. *Teacher Education Quarterly*. Caddo Gap Press. HighBeam Research. Available online at: **www.highbeam.com**.

Vygotsky, LS (1966) Genesis of the Higher Mental Functions, in Light, P, Sheldon, S and Woodhead, M (eds) (1991) *Learning to Think*. London: Routledge.

Wallace, D (2006) *The Learning Engine: Building Capabilities Through Communities of Practice. (Communities of Practice). Information Outlook*. Special Libraries Association. HighBeam Research. Available online at: **www.highbeam.com**.

Wild, M and Mitchell, H (eds) (2007) *Early Childhood Studies, a Reflective Reader*. Exeter: Learning Matters.

Willan, J (2004) in Willan, J, Parker-Rees, R and Savage, J (eds) *Early Childhood Studies*. Exeter: Learning Matters.

Wood, D (1986) Aspects of Teaching and Learning, in Light, P, Sheldon, S and Woodhead, M (eds) (1991) *Learning to Think*. London: Routledge.

Zimitat, C (2007) Capturing Community of Practice Knowledge for Student Learning. *Innovations in Education and Teaching International*. HighBeam Research. Available online at: **www.highbeam.com**.

WEBSITES

www.teachernet.gov.uk

www.tda.gov.uk

www.cwdcouncil.org.uk/eypsfutures

3 The placement experience

Nicky Hirst and Elaine Hodson

CHAPTER OBJECTIVES

By the end of this chapter you should:

- *have an understanding of the expectations of a placement;*
- *have an awareness of the complex nature of the student experience;*
- *have a developing awareness of strategies available to support you in meeting the demands of the placement.*

This chapter addresses the following Professional Standards for QTS and EYPS:
QTS: Q1; 2; 3; 4; 5; 6; 7; 8; 9; 32; 33.
EYPS: S 33; 34; 35; 36; 37; 38; 39.

Introduction

The aim of this chapter is to support you in getting the most out of your experience on placement. Your placement experience will provide you with a 'real' context to help you make sense of the connections between theory, policy and practice. If you have followed the guidance from the previous chapter, you should now be in a position where you are fully aware of your own responsibilities and course requirements. This chapter helps you to consider the importance of the establishment of effective relationships with the children and practitioners who work in your placement setting. It will explain the roles of the staff involved in your ongoing assessment and will support you in setting and meeting your personal targets and in dealing with any possible challenges.

Establishing relationships, roles, responsibilities and expectations

Chapter 1 provided you with a sense of the historical and political context for Early Years provision, and the particular uniqueness of each sector. While in your placement, you will begin to understand the way ECM is implemented in practice. Your Early Years placement is responsible for delivering the EYFS and is inspected against the five ECM outcomes, that ensure that each child is:

- healthy;

- safe;

- enjoys life;

- makes a positive contribution;

- achieves economic well-being.

(**www.everychildmatters.gov.uk/aims**)

In order to ensure the best possible outcomes for children, the legislation is based on a commitment to the integration of all involved services. Effective high quality communication is seen to be the key to this effectiveness, and part of your role will be your commitment to this. You will be expected to work as part of a team, share information, and work together to protect, care for, and teach the children in your setting. In this safe environment, children will be encouraged to achieve and to begin to make decisions. You may be surprised at the enthusiasm shown by even very young children when they are given the opportunity to influence decisions about issues that impact directly on them.

Induction into placement

As a student you will start your placement safe in the knowledge that you are a *suitable person* (Statutory framework for the EYFS, 2008, page 29). Initially, you may feel that you are an outsider entering a new and exciting world. Lave and Wenger (1991, page 100)) describe this position as, *legitimate peripherality*. They use the term 'peripheral' in a positive manner. They argue that, as a student, you are not *disconnected* (page 37) from practice but that you are learning through access to sources of support. In turn, these sources will help you to develop your understanding. It may be worth here thinking about the impact of your first days and how you can establish those relationships by utilising the professional support and advice on offer.

When you join a setting you become a member of an established team, it is essential that you find out the roles and responsibilities of all staff within the placement. It is particularly important that you identify the Special Educational Needs Co-ordinator (SENCO), as this particular member of staff will be a vital source of support, able to discuss children's needs and show you Individual Education Plans (IEPs). Remember you will also need to introduce yourself to others! Colleagues will need to know about the programme you are on and its expectations if they are to be able to support you. It is worth reminding yourself that people will be keen to help you to achieve your goals. Your mentor (refer to Chapter 2) has a particular responsibility to help you, but they will also draw on the expertise of others to ensure that you are able to access all the specialist support available.

Chapter 2 discussed Lave and Wenger's (1991) assertion that physicality is an essential factor in developing a community of practice. This factor highlights the need for you to maintain a professional approach through consistent and punctual attendance. Remember, informing the placement of any domestic arrangements is simply common courtesy and demonstrates a professional attitude to the experience. A professional placement is a serious undertaking and carries serious commitments. Your training provider will have a minimum attendance requirement, but it is worth reminding yourself that placement experience is both valuable and necessary. Even negative experiences will be developmental. A positive outlook and a 'glass half full' approach will help you to learn from the most challenging events.

Within your placement there will be an expectation that you will embrace the ethos and working practices particular to that context. Therefore, access to information will be a key component in your success. Chapter 2 suggests some valuable strategies for gaining this information and emphasises the need to be prepared. Possessing information relevant to this new situation will place you in a better position to protect, prepare and provide for yourself, to make considered judgements and to demonstrate competency in your role. In essence, information *empowers* people, while a lack of pertinent information has the opposite effect (Rodd, 2006).

Lave and Wenger's (1991) notion of a community of practice suggests that learning involves a progressively deepening process of participation within the culture of a 'community'. Similarly, Stacey (2009, page 79) points out that this social learning through *participation and collaboration with others* occurs in both children and adults. This collaboration will form a major part of your placement experience as you involve yourself in a set of sustained interactions with various people. Whether you are placed in a non-maintained or PVI setting (see Chapter 1 for clarification of examples), a Children's Centre or a maintained sector nursery or Reception class, it is a statutory requirement that you not only have access to policies and procedures, but that they are explained and accessible as part of an induction process (DCSF, 2008, page 20). This will enable you to:

• understand how policy works within day-to-day practice;

• develop a shared responsibility;

• influence development by prompting others to reflect on their personal or group interpretation of existing policy;

• gain autonomy and a sense of ownership in a safe environment;

• set targets for your own progress.

Schools are not required to have *separate* policies for the EYFS (EYFS, 2008) provided that the requirements are met through their policies which cover children of statutory school age. Therefore, it is important that you read and discuss the implementation of whole school policy in your practice context. You will then be able to make some explicit and coherent links to the principles and content of the EYFS.

PRACTICAL TASK

Look at section three of the Welfare Requirements section of the Statutory Framework for the Early Years Foundation Stage *(2008, pages 19-40) and consider the implications for your practice as a student on placement:*

• *How can you check your understanding is shared with others in the setting?*

• *What personal responsibility will you need to undertake?*

• *Think how you might begin to 'evidence' your development in this area.*

CHALLENGES and DILEMMAS

As a student you need to develop a sense of ownership over your placement experience. Read the case study below:

Philippa approached her first professional placement on the Early Years Professional Status 'Full' pathway. She was unsure what to expect but had read her handbook and had listened attentively to her tutors at university. When she arrived at placement, the manager of the pre-school informed Philippa that there was 'no time for an induction' as she was very busy. As the week went by Philippa noted that she needed to know about the policies and procedures of the placement before she could understand how the setting worked. She spoke to her placement mentor and requested copies of the policies and procedures and was offered the opportunity to read through the documents in her own time.

Philippa looked at the policies and made a note to discuss, observe and ask questions as her placement progressed. She made a conscious decision to be proactive and find out who was responsible for children with SEN and she spoke to the setting's SENCO. Philippa used a reflective journal to make notes in an informal way and she ensured that staff felt reassured about the content of any formal entries. She saw this note taking as a valuable way to build up a comprehensive picture of the way the setting worked.

While noting the busy workload of practitioners within her placement, Philippa considered how she could use this experience to enhance her own knowledge, understanding and leadership skills, therefore she asked if she could contribute to an induction pack for new students coming into the setting. This instigated discussions regarding policies and practice in a collaborative way. Philippa located the behaviour policy and used her emerging understanding to consider her own behaviour and how this may influence the behaviour of others within her placement. This highly motivated and conscientious attitude formed the basis for further exploration.

Phillippa concluded from her reading of the behaviour policy that it implied an approach that encapsulated equality, reflection and a lack of hierarchical positions in terms of adult status. The pre-school was an independent setting but shared the policy with the Reception class of a maintained school. She made a note to suggest that she spent some time later in the Reception class to observe its implementation in that contrasting setting.

Establishing your responsibilities and role

Chapter 2 highlighted the interchangeable language used to describe the roles of the different people associated with your placement experience. It would be wise at this point, to ensure that you have a clear understanding of the procedures associated with your particular training programme; for example, the frequency and timing of practice observations, opportunity for mentoring, and the arrangements for assessment. It is then your responsibility to be proactive and to discuss this early in the placement. Uncertainties on all sides can then be aired, and you will be seen to be exhibiting the professional attitude expected of you.

Whatever the context, you will be expected to arrive with the following:

- A developing awareness of the demands of your programme or the standards for QTS/EYPS.

- The relevant handbooks and associated documentation.

- A sound understanding of your targets for this placement.

- A positive and professional approach.

The preparation outlined in Chapter 2 is highly likely to pay dividends as you establish a sense of purpose within your setting. Although at times preparation may appear cumbersome, now is the time that you will reap the rewards. Being able to articulate personal beliefs and a sound rationale for your choice of course will help you to develop self-awareness. It is worth remembering that many practitioners you will be working with are both well-qualified for their role and particularly experienced. You may be feeling both intimidated and eager, but will now need to consider how you can utilise this expertise. Knowledgeable members of staff are far more likely to share their ideas with you if you talk to them and explain what it is you are intending to achieve. Remember that working towards your qualification does not mean that you are in competition with those in other roles, but that you too are learning to work within a professional context.

On all courses you will be expected, with varying methods of support, to set targets for your placement. These targets will be discussed and appropriately documented. All weekly reports, formative and summative assessments and any possible observations of practice will be focused on these targets and provide evidence of your progress. Remember that 'evidence' is gained through a process of mutual understanding and assessment and is not simply something that is *done to you*, rather *for* and *with you* (Boud, 1988). Indeed, the QTS standard (Q9), requires that a trainee should, *act upon advice and feedback and be open to coaching and mentoring* and similarly, the standards for EYPS highlight the requirement for *reflective practitioners* (Stds 37–39). Considered in that way, you will see yourself as one of a range of stakeholders involved in a process of quality assurance.

In Chapter 2 we considered the SMART target-setting model. Now speak to your mentor and suggest how you might take responsibility to review your collection of evidence of progress by using a goal-setting model. This draws on the acronym ACHIEVE (see Table 3.1).

Legitimising membership and meaningful involvement

As you gain some perspective of yourself as a budding professional, it will be important to consider where you think you are and what you need to achieve. For example, you will need to review your values and your attitude to teaching and caring for young children, clarifying to yourself exactly what is important to you and why. If you believe that young children learn best through first-hand experience and in a social context, then now is the time to begin to think about why you feel this way and how this will impact on the decisions you make.

A	Ability	How will you acquire the necessary skills and knowledge?
C	Clarity	What do you want to achieve and why?
H	Help	What assistance do you need? Where will you find it and who will help you?
I	Implementation Plan	What steps need to be taken? What is your time frame?
E	Environment	How will the placement support achievement of your goals?
V	Values	Will your personal values help or hinder your professional practice?
E	Evidence	How will you know when a goal has been reached?

Table 3.1 Action plan for achievement

CHALLENGES and DILEMMAS

Although policies are a statutory requirement, practitioner interpretation of, for example, a behaviour policy, is important for you to understand. Medwell (2008) talks about the school behaviour policy in terms of setting the scene, giving you a feeling of the ethos and behaviour within the context and the relationships that staff hope to establish and maintain. The behaviour policy used within your placement will provide an insight for you as a student of the strategies used by all practitioners.

Policies and procedures are only meaningful if the principles underpinning them are mirrored within practice. It is worth remembering that the policy documents you read, both prior to, and during your placement experience, represent the 'how to' element within the Statutory Framework (EYFS, 2008). In terms of expectations, you may not always see policy translated into daily practice. However, questions you raise and suggestions you make will be valuable in bringing a fresh set of eyes to a situation. This may well result in an opportunity for reflection for the whole team as they review their practice. The following two scenarios illustrate contrasting ways in which practitioners interpret the behaviour policy of a setting, and should help you to consider how your 'fresh eyes' may help a team develop a consistent approach to behaviour management.

Scenario one

Anna is a qualified level three practitioner who is working in the pre-school context. She appears to have a good rapport with the children who are evidently happy in her care, and you are eager to learn by watching her interactions with them while you are on placement. Whenever you hear Anna responding to a challenging situation with a child, she regularly cajoles with comments that appear to be contradictory to the policy ethos, by deferring to senior members of staff, for example, 'if you don't tidy the toys away Mrs X will be cross'. Furthermore, Anna's message appears to be confusing for the children

continued

37

as she clears resources away while demanding their input in an increasingly loud and agitated voice! You consider ways that you could help the children to be more independent by placing the toys away themselves and you make a note to discuss this with staff.

Scenario two

Sophie is a teaching assistant (TA) in a Reception class of a large primary school. Her relationship with the children in the class appears to be based on a shared understanding of boundaries and acceptable behaviour. From your observations, you note that she appears to work in harmony with the class teacher and the children are aware of the excellent partnership approach. You have noted that the children spend a considerable amount of time moving around the class in a harmonious way, however, you also observe the transitional period from child led activities within the role play area to 'carpet time' instigates an onslaught of 'silly behaviour' for which the boys in particular are reprimanded. Further observation highlights the difficulties with this transition where the adult 'request' is hurried and the children appear to be reacting to this in a negative way. You have read the behaviour policy of the setting and you are in the privileged position of 'seeing' any problems with a fresh pair of eyes. You consider a simple strategy that may help to redefine the children's status by allowing them the autonomy to bring closure to their game. Your idea of a large sand timer as a visual reminder that 'any monsters will need to get ready for carpet time when the sand has run through the timer' needs to be discussed in a collegiate manner.

A balancing act: your role as a team player and course expectations

In all EYFS settings, young children are supported in their learning and development. Your position as a student quickly places you in the midst of this learning. Children do not differentiate between 'the student' and other adults. It will be your attitude, as much as that of your experienced colleagues, that will help to determine the ground rules for behaviour *for* their learning (Adams, 2009).

Using **scenario one** to guide your thinking;

The guidance to the Standards for the Award of Early Years Professional Status (2008, page 5) states that:

> *EYPs are catalysts for change and innovation: they are key to raising the quality of early years provision and exercise leadership in making a positive difference to children's well-being, learning and development ...*

The word 'leadership' itself is a slippery concept and one that is widely debated in terms of the student experience; however, as a student you will draw on a 'repertoire of strategies' to lead others in their thinking. You will need to be sure that discussions are carried on in a sensitive way.

Given that learning and behaviour are inextricably linked, think how you can use this behaviour policy to lead discussion about ways, as a team, you might increase the children's learning opportunities when tidying away the resources.

Bearing this in mind:

- Who would you need to discuss any ideas with?

- Can you provide a sound rationale for your ideas and have you any observations to substantiate your ideas?

- How are the principles of the EYFS reflected in your practice?

- Modeling practice could be a positive starting point but are you clear about your intentions?

- How could you evidence any possible changes for your summative assessment?

Using **scenario two** to guide your thinking;

There are very particular expectations for you as a trainee, as you will be in effect taking over a class from someone who will inevitably already have a sense of professional 'ownership' and commitment to those children. The class teacher will expect you to be consultative about possible changes to practice.

- Consider your commitment to ensuring 'high expectations' for the children in your care, ask yourself how you interpret this requirement in the context of classroom practices.

- Consider *the difficulties associated with teaching in another person's classroom and the complexities of aligning your approach and practice to fit with their expectations* (Hayes 2009, page 26).

- Consider how as a developing teacher you will gradually take responsibility for the planning and delivery of the EYFS in this classroom and the deployment of other adults in the class, such as teaching assistants like Sophie, parents, volunteers and visiting professionals. Hayes (2009, page 47) talks about trainees needing to treat teaching assistants with *great courtesy*. How will you ensure you are courteous to others?

- How will you gather some understanding of the role of a teaching assistant to help you to contextualise their responsibilities and build respectful, reciprocal relationships?

According to Walton and Goddard (2009, page 19) the TDA considers support staff to be *at the heart of social reform particularly with the emergence of the new Higher Level Teaching Assistant (HLTA) and specialist roles*. Hayes (2009, page 48) reminds us of the importance of a strong collegiate approach and that this relationship influences your role as a trainee in terms of how roles and responsibilities in the classroom are allocated.

Bearing this in mind:

- How would you share your ideas for the transition period with both the teacher and the TA?

- What would your rationale be and how could you 'sell' this idea in a confident but sensitive manner?

- How are the principles of the EYFS reflected in your practice?

- How could you collect 'evidence' from this process for discussions with your mentor?

Making the most of feedback and assessment

Preparation for mentor assessments will be essential and will demonstrate your attitude to your personal professional development. Utilising feedback (both verbal and written) will demonstrate a positive and committed response. The cultivation of the capacity to reflect in action (while you are engaged in an activity or experience with a group of children) and on action (after you have done it) has become an important feature of professional training programmes in different disciplines. It is part of your mentor's role to help you to make sense of experiences and to make links in your learning. The discussions that you have are, therefore, very important. In their discussion surrounding mentoring and coaching, Garvey, Stokes and Megginson (2009) remind us that Vygotsky viewed dialogic (learning through discussion) as *higher mental function*. It is worth reminding yourself of the significance of these meetings for negotiating a shared understanding of what consti-tutes 'evidence' of progress. Your learning is not an activity simply occurring in isolation. Vygotsky (1978) maintains that all human learning occurs through a social interaction. It might help you to consider that the process of collaboration with your mentor is not far removed from the negotiated learning you may have heard associated with Reggio Emilia (Forman and Fyfe, in Edwards et al., 1998, page 239). To enable parallels to be drawn with your placement experience, negotiated learning could be considered in terms of your work with both children and with other adults.

Consider the learning involved in your placement experience in terms of the 'zone of proximal development', described as *the distance between the actual development level as determined by independent problem solving and the level of potential develop-ment as determined through problem solving...in collaboration with more capable peers* (Vygotsky,1978). The implication for your discussions with your mentor is that under-standing and learning is achieved through dialogue and collaboration. Phil Race suggests that other people's 'knowledge' is just information. However, he argues that mentoring can transform that information into knowledge through supporting the extension and interrogation and application of a trainee's ideas.

REFLECTIVE TASK

Consider the following examples that constitute a reflective approach and an opportunity for informed dialogue with your mentor. The scenarios from the previous section have been used to demonstrate a proactive, timely and relevant approach.

*In order to **judge** how prepared you are for a mentor meeting you will need to **consider**:*

- *your reflection on your targets;*
- *your response to any feedback from mentors/tutors;*
- *the preparation of any documentary 'evidence' (paperwork, observations, planning, notes from meetings);*
- *the assessment criteria.*

Example (taken from scenario one)

Having read the behaviour policy, I feel that I have gained a better understanding of the ethos of this placement. It is apparent to me that 'policy' into practice can be problematic and that as a student I need to negotiate a way to share ideas with existing staff. I have been modelling what I hope is positive practice, hoping that the staff in the room will see that there are other ways to engage the children in 'tidy up' time. I have asked the room leader if it would be possible to trial a new idea where the children are given respon- sibility for tidying different areas. I have read that children respond well to being given responsibility and that their behaviour is merely a response to variable factors. This would sit comfortably with the principle of the behaviour policy and allow all staff to facilitate this independence.

Placement mentor feedback

'X' has considered her role as a student and has demonstrated a sensitive approach to developing the behaviour policy into practice (S17, 35). Observations of practice in the pre-school room demonstrated how 'X' modelled practice including her discussions with the children regarding 'tidy up time' (S28). She spent time listening to children and scribed their ideas onto a large piece of paper to create their own rules for tidying up (S27). She talked to the staff in the room about the children's independence and together they came up with some new ideas to create a more inclusive and child-centred approach (S33). She identified areas of learning for the children and hoped to discuss this with staff at the next planning meeting (S7, 34).

Possible future targets arrived at in discussion with your mentor:

- Attend the next staff meeting and consider how you can extend and develop these ideas (S33, 34).
- Review the pictures displayed on the behaviour policy triangle (displayed in the room) to include photographs of the children tidying up (S35, 37).
- Discuss the concept of Continuous Provision and the implications for practice at the next staff meeting (S4, 35).
- Grasp the opportunity to make contact with parents and carers and find out about the mechanisms for sharing information with them (S29-32).

Example (taken from scenario two)

I observed the Reception class and noticed that the relationship between the TA and the teacher was really strong. I was particularly nervous about taking over this class but used my observations to share with the staff. They had also noticed that the transition from 'free play' activities to 'carpet time' was disjointed and they welcomed my idea of a visual reminder.

I used the time to discuss my ideas with the TA as I will be working closely with her when I take over the class. I used the visual element of the behaviour policy (displayed in the room) to talk to the children about this transition.

Placement mentor feedback

I observed 'X' in the classroom where she used the visual element of the behaviour policy to discuss the transition periods with the children (Q1) and she used this developmentally appropriate discussion to develop their thinking in terms of fairness and attitude (Q2). 'X' has demonstrated a working knowledge and understanding of the behaviour policy and has contributed to its implementation by adapting a small but relevant element of practice in the classroom (Q3a,3b).

Possible future targets arrived at in discussion with your mentor:

● Think how you can develop the opportunity to discuss this change with parents and carers (Q4).

● Familiarise yourself with the planning formats within the EYFS and plan a series of sustained activities demonstrating how each of the six areas of learning will be addressed (Q4).

Documenting your response to placement mentor feedback

Feedback is essential to help you to move forward. It can be a powerful tool to help you to feel a sense of achievement. The ultimate goal for any mentor is to enable you as a student to self-assess and to appreciate when you have gained 'self- knowledge' (to know what you stand for, to clarify your principles and to cope and respond to any uncertainties). Your response to feedback will be a key feature of any assessment. You will need to show how any feedback has enabled you to move forward. Now is also the time to celebrate your achievements (either personal or collaborative). You will need to:

● make notes in your reflective journal or diary;

● colour code any links to the relevant standards;

● use any self-review documentation to discuss with your mentor;

● complete any documentation in a timely manner to show your mentor that you value their support and professional perspective.

Gathering evidence for external assessors is essential for summative assessment of your competency, therefore it is worth spending time considering how this can be achieved. Using scenario one as an example you would need to collect:

● ongoing observations of the children's behaviour at the identified period;

● records of the children's ideas and how these were interpreted into practice;

● any observation, assessment and/or planning;

● minutes from staff meetings with clear objectives and responsibilities;

● reviews of the photographic representations of the behaviour policy both for and with the children;

● letters or notices for parents.

'Evidence' versus 'proof'

The requisite requirement to gain 'evidence' while on placement will vary according to your training route or programme of study. However, it is important to consider the difference in terms of ideology, to distinguish between 'evidence' and 'proof'. Hayes (2009) discusses this difference:

Evidence that teaching standards have been satisfactorily met is gained through a process of (a) the student teacher demonstrating competence, together with (b) a tutor or teacher confirming that the evidence is valid. It is important to note that evidence is not the same as proof. Whereas evidence allows for professional judgement, discussion and flexibility, proof is absolute, with no room for manoeuvre.

(Hayes, 2009, page 7)

The following examples of self-review notepads would provide the opportunity to review and discuss progress with a mentor and could be regularly annotated and updated, and then revised to include all standards.

Example: EYP STANDARDS SELF-REVIEW NOTEPAD

This document could be used as a notebook to aid your exploration of the Standards and the ways in which you can meet each one. You will find it helpful to refer to your copy of the Guidance to the Standards related to your course (EYPS) and you may also find it helpful to note any questions you want to ask your mentor or tutor about a specific Standard.

Std.	Description	Comments and Queries
KNOWLEDGE AND UNDERSTANDING		
Those awarded Early Years Professional Status must demonstrate through their practice that a secure knowledge and understanding underpins their own practice and informs their leadership of others. This knowledge and understanding is reflected in Standards S1–S6, each of which can be demonstrated through candidates' practice.		
S1	The principles and content of the Early Years Foundation Stage and how to put them into practice	*I am constantly referring to the practice guidance for the EYFS and have introduced a more independent method for the children to tidy toys away. I can make the connections to the six areas of learning and can discuss this with the staff. Now I feel I need to involve everyone in devising more ideas and embed the principles into practice. Speak to Jayne to discuss possible strategies.*
S2	The individual and diverse ways in which children develop and learn from birth to the end of the Foundation Stage and thereafter	*I can see how children are all different and I have studied the Unique Child section of the EYFS. I can see the broad developmental 'stages', however I need to speak to Jayne about how to use my observations to inform this understanding.*

S3	How children's well-being, development, learning and behaviour can be affected by a range of influences and transitions from inside and outside the setting	*I have used my observations to improve the transitional phases within the daily routine but I need to acknowledge the possible influences of a child's home life. I need to talk to Jayne and see how I can develop further opportunities to talk to parents and carers.*
S4	The main provisions of the national and local statutory and non-statutory frameworks within which children's services work and their implications for Early Years settings	*I think I am gaining a working knowledge of the EYFS, however it would be good to discuss with staff their interpretation of the planning for the individual child. How can I do this with the ratios in the room? Speak to Jayne.*
S5	The current legal requirements, national policies and guidance on health and safety, safeguarding and promoting the well-being of children and their implications for Early Years settings	*I have read some of the policies and procedures and know the safeguarding procedure of the setting. I would like to take the sensory play idea into the outside area but I'll need to check the risk assessment and staff ratios.*
S6	The contribution that other professionals within the setting and beyond can make to children's physical and emotional well-being, development and learning	*I am unsure of the different professionals working within placement. Maybe I could discuss the rationale for my sensory experiences with the health visitor or the speech and language therapist to gain more knowledge and understanding and different perspectives.*

The end of the placement

The conclusion of a placement experience is not the end of the story. Now is the time to summarise what you have learned and see what you can take forward.

In her article 'Dimensions of Early Years professionalism – attitudes versus competences?' Avril Brock (www.tactyc.org.uk) suggests that care is needed with the emphasis surrounding the need to acquire 'standards' and competencies, rather than considering what might constitute professionalism. She articulates her concern that in an attempt to 'achieve' and 'do their best' professionals working in the Early Years will interpret the standards *as they are stated* (page 6). Basford (2008, page 4) suggests that it is important that you begin to develop your own philosophy, which may change either subtly or dramatically as you gain more experience.

An important element will be to thank all staff who have supported you and to demonstrate a genuine gratitude for their hard work or commitment. The end of a placement can bring with it an array of emotional responses, particularly where students have made positive relationships with staff and children. It is important not to let any emotion run away with you and maintain the professionalism associated with your training. Dissolving into tears with a group of very young children could be distressing for them. Leaving any placement brings what Medwell (2008) describes as *a duty of confidentiality,* where you will need to remain alert to your responsibilities to the children. Social networking sites are popular and are often seductive in their promise of maintaining friendships, however, a good rule of thumb is that nothing should be posted electronically which would not be said in any other public forum. Remember, you never know who may have access to information published on internet sites. Photographs of children must, of course, **never** be posted onto such sites.

C H A P T E R   S U M M A R Y

This chapter has provided an overview of the complex nature of the placement experience. The success of your placement will be greatly influenced by the extent to which you are able to build positive and professional relationships with both the staff and children of the setting. Your placement provides you with the unique opportunity to make connections between theory, policy and practice. By reflecting on your experience, you may well learn new things about yourself, but you will also confirm some of your own ideas about working with children and families. You will most probably be engaged in some form of assessment and feedback related to your own competencies as an Early Years practitioner. In order to gain the most from this process it is important that you take responsibility for your own professional development. Organisation, honesty and commitment are the key to a successful placement.

REFERENCES

Adams, K (2009) *Behaviour for Learning in the Primary School.* Exeter: Learning Matters.

Basford, J and Hodson, E (2008) *Teaching Early Years Foundation Stage.* Exeter: Learning Matters.

Boud, D (1988) *Developing Student Autonomy* (2nd ed). London: Kogan Page.

Children's Workforce Development Council (CWDC) (2008) *Guidance for Early Years Professional Status.* Leeds: CWDC.

DCSF (2008) *Statutory Framework for the Early Years Foundation Stage.* London: DCSF.

DfES (2004) *Every Child Matters: Change for Children.* London: DfES.

Edwards, C, Gandini, L and Forman, G (1998) *The Hundred Languages of Children; The Reggio Approach – Advanced Reflections.* London: Ablex Publishing.

Garvey, R, Stokes, P and Megginson, D (2009) *Coaching and Mentoring: Theory and Practice.* London: Sage.

Hayes, D (2009) *Learning and Teaching in Primary Schools.* Exeter: Learning Matters.

Lave, J and Wenger, E (1991) *Situated Learning: Legitimate Peripheral Participation.* Cambridge: Cambridge University Press.

Medwell, J (2008) *Successful Teaching Placement: Primary and Early Years*. Exeter: Learning Matters.

Rodd, J (2006) *Leadership in Early Childhood*. Maidenhead: Open University Press.

Stacey, M (2009) *Teamwork and Collaboration in Early Years Settings*. Exeter: Learning Matters.

Vygotsky, LS (1978) *Mind in Society*. Cambridge MA: Harvard University Press.

Walton, A and Goddard, G (2009) *Supporting Every Child*. Exeter: Learning Matters.

Wenger, E (1998) *Communities of Practice: Learning, Meaning, and Identity*. Cambridge: Cambridge University Press.

Adams, K (2009) *Behaviour for Learning in the Primary School*. Exeter: Learning Matters.

Brock, A (2006) *Dimensions of Early Years Professionalism – Attitudes Versus Competences?* Leeds: Leeds Metropolitan University Publications.

http://phil-race.co.uk

4 A unique child

Sue van Gaalen

CHAPTER OBJECTIVES

By the end of this chapter you should:

- *understand the holistic and unique nature of a child's development;*
- *understand how inclusive practice supports every child's entitlement to high quality provision;*
- *have an awareness of health and safety issues and the importance of promoting safeguarding principles.*

This chapter addresses the following Professional Standards for QTS and EYPS:
QTS: Q1; 2; 5; 10; 18; 19; 20; 21(a), (b).
EYPS: S2; 3; 5; 14; 18; 19; 20; 21; 23; 28; 29; 31.

Introduction

It is intended that this chapter will help you consider your developing understanding of the EYFS commitment to treat every child as a unique individual, and the way your placement experience will support you in this. As some placements are quite short, and it may take you time to get to know children, the chapter will make suggestions for strategies to help overcome this. The chapter will be relevant whether the placement is in a PVI Early Years setting or a maintained nursery or Reception class.

Katz (1993) suggests that practitioners should look through the eyes of a child in a setting and ask some basic questions:

- Do I feel welcome?

- Do I belong?

- Am I usually accepted and understood?

These could perhaps be summed up in the one question:

- Am I being treated as a unique child?

This philosophy is central to current thinking on child-centred learning in England since, as Smidt describes, in the western world, child development studies are,

> *characterised by the notion of the ideal child as an individual. We are used to considering the importance of each child – thinking about each child's preferences,*

fears, experiences, strengths and weaknesses. Educators in the developed world
promote ideas of self-confidence and self-esteem, separateness and individuality.

(Smidt, 2006 page 28)

The chapter adopts the headings from the EYFS theme, A Unique Child, and is intended to make these ideas accessible to you during your placement experience.

Child development

There has been considerable debate over recent years about the validity of an 'ages and stages' view of child development. It is now generally recognised that such an enormous variation exists within the range of 'normal' development, for example some children may walk as young as nine months while others do not begin until fifteen months or later. Therefore, any suggestion of 'normality' is not only unhelpful, but may cause unnecessary anxiety to parents and practitioners. Current thinking acknowledges that every child will develop in their own way and at their own pace, and as Smidt (2006) states, it is a *continuous and cumulative process.* While you are in a placement you will be required to provide appropriate activities to support children's learning and development. In order to do this, you need to have an understanding of how best to match this to their current levels of achievement (you will find more detailed discussion of this in Chapter 7). The EYFS Practice Guidance states that *every area of development – physical, cognitive, linguistic, spiritual, social and emotional, is equally important,* and this is supported by findings from the EPPE study (Sylva et al., 2004, page 2) which identified that *where settings view educational and social development as complimentary and equal in importance, children make better all round progress.*

However, within this particular commitment, the EYFS pays particular attention to the child as a **competent learner**, and **skilful communicator**. This terminology takes its origins from the *Birth to Three Matters* framework (DfES, 2002), a seminal document which helped practitioners to challenge traditional notions of describing development in separate domains, and instead to view children in a holistic and multidimensional way, where they are acknowledged as having personalities, thoughts, emotions, ideas, skills and dispositions – from birth (Abbot and Langston, 2005). The particular emphasis on the child as being both a learner and communicator should help you to see the vital connection between language and thinking. Children's learning is influenced by their interactions with their environment, and the people who exist within it. Further reference is made to this in Chapters 5 and 7.

Tasks set for you to complete during your placement may involve you in making observations or studies of a particular child. This is a key tool used by practitioners to help not only to plan for future learning (as explored in further detail in Chapter 6), but to help consider different aspects of children's development. We have already acknowledged that there are many different theoretical viewpoints related to child development, and the philosophical stance a practitioner takes can influence the way individual children are viewed.

Nutbrown states that:

> Whatever the national policy, practitioners' own personal and professional values underpin their assessment practices. Those who work with young children bring to the processes of assessment their implicit values and their beliefs about children … the ways in which adults assess children depend upon their views on the nature of childhood, children's behaviour, children's feelings and their personal approaches to living and learning. Whenever, wherever educators observe, assess and interpret young children's learning, they are influenced by personal beliefs and values.
>
> (Nutbrown, 2006, page 100)

At the same time you will also be required to consider the individual needs of all the other children you will be working with. Information can be gained from children's files (ensuring you have consent to do so first!). The files should include details of any special educational need and any individual plans for children such as Individual Education Plans (IEPs), Individual Behaviour Plans (IBPs) or Personal Education Plans (PEPs) for Looked After Children (LAC). All this information is confidential and you must be prepared to give the setting reassurance that you, as a student, understand the sensitive nature of this information. (This issue is discussed in detail in Chapters 2 and 3.)

When planning for individual children, it is important to make the connection between 'the Unique Child' and 'starting with the child' (see Chapter 6 for more detail). Your settings may use Possible Lines of Direction (PLODs) as a starting point for planning experiences for children and these will be invaluable to help you plan for individual needs. They will have been created by practitioners after completing observations and will note such things as: possible schemas that the child may be exhibiting; personal interests; or particular skills or talents. Each child's key person (see Chapter 5) will be the significant person who is able to discuss him or her in detail. Read (2010) states that the role of the key person can be central to *creating a unique relationship with a child and family and young children having their individual needs met.* It is often possible to speak with parents about their children's interests, and of course, spending time with the children themselves will give you an insight into their unique characteristics and temperament. *The ability to read young children's behaviour and to communicate with them is at the basis of successful practice* (Dowling, 2005). A good question to ask colleagues before you start working with *any* group of children is 'Is there anything I need to know?' This can prove vital. For example, one student was made aware of a child who was part of a Protected Witness Scheme. As a result, no photographs were to be taken of her, even for use within the setting. You may also be made aware of medical conditions such as epilepsy or allergies or restrictions about collection arrangements. Do not presume that you will be told everything you need to know, remember to ask questions and to be proactive.

Inclusive practice

The EYFS states that:

> Children should be treated fairly regardless of race, religion or abilities. This applies no matter what they think or say; what type of family they come from; what language(s) they speak; what their parents do; whether they are girls or boys; whether they have a disability or whether they are rich or poor.
>
> (DCSF, 2008)

This has to be a philosophy that underpins all practice and provision, rather than existing as an afterthought. Truly inclusive practice will be evident to you in a setting, but you will need to look for more than a box in the staffroom marked 'Festivals' and a poster in the entrance hall that welcomes visitors in a variety of languages. It is part of your role to look at the resources available to the children and ask yourself if the resources reflect the children's home experiences. Look at the clothes available or food and utensils on offer in the role play area. Think about the range of books and pictures on display around the setting. Baldock (2010) suggests that although a setting may have a range of resources from different cultures, it is the way that they are used that is important, and their *presence does not prove all is well*. He suggests that it is useful to start by introducing to children aspects of a different culture that they can relate to, such as food, music or celebrations, but practitioners will also need to understand the significance of items in that culture. Most festivals, for example,

> have a religious origin. To celebrate one of them is to raise issues of belief. This can be difficult for white people who are not practising Christians to understand, since in the United Kingdom the major festivals have become detached in the minds of many from their faith origins.

> (Baldock, 2010, page 74)

You need to be aware when setting up displays that it may be offensive to show some religious texts or artefacts outside an explicit faith context. Baldock (2010) and Sylva and Siraj-Blatchford (1996) agree on the importance of including parents in explaining aspects of their own cultures. Children and their parents *bring to the school a wealth of cultural, linguistic and economic experience which the school can call upon* (Siraj-Blatchford, 2001 page 107).

The EYFS states:

> Inclusion is about attitudes as well as behaviour and practices. The attitudes of young children towards diversity are affected by the behaviour of adults around them and by whether all children and families using the setting are valued and welcomed. Inclusive settings recognise and celebrate diversity.

> (DCFS, 2008)

PRACTICAL TASK

Spend some time thinking about the way you might develop your practice by improving your own awareness of diversity. Make some notes about some actions that would help you with this.

You might begin by researching a faith that you are not currently familiar with. What are the main beliefs – are there any dietary or clothing obligations? How might these affect a child's experience in an Early Years setting?

Every child will come to the setting or school with a unique set of experiences which will need to be valued by all practitioners and students. Therefore, it is important that:

- you have a knowledge and understanding of the different cultural backgrounds of the children who you will be meeting;

- you ensure that all the resources you use are free from negative stereotyping and reflect the diversity of Britain today;

- you have an understanding of the context of a child's life, their position in the family, the languages spoken at home and so forth. A child coming from a large family may, for example, have learnt to be assertive and have a very different concept of sharing from an only child who has never had to relinquish toys to others or to vie for attention. However, it is also important not to make assumptions, the singleton may have had lots of experience of being with other children, perhaps through being in childcare settings, or having spent a considerable time with extended family or friends.

The EYFS states that:

Practitioners should plan to meet the needs of both boys and girls, children with special educational needs, children who are more able, children with disabilities, children with complex health needs, children from all social, family, cultural and religious backgrounds, looked after children, children of all ethnic groups including traveller communities, refugee and asylum seekers and children from diverse linguistic backgrounds.

(DCSF, 2008)

This list, though extensive, is not fully comprehensive, and you should bear in mind that there will always be children who fall outside this range but also have the right to have their needs met. For example, an adopted child may have had a difficult early life experience, and while is not a LAC, may need some additional understanding of their needs.

It is also important to consider the concept of equality of opportunity. This does not mean that all children must have the same opportunity, but each child must be able to access opportunities in ways that are appropriate for their needs. Although a SENCO or bilingual support worker may have a specialist role, everyone working with children has a part to play and responsibility to ensure that every child feels valued and has the opportunity to achieve their potential. Children who have a disability or a special learning need may require more adult help to be able to fully participate in an activity. This should be borne in mind when you are planning and preparing. For example, if you are planning for other adults, you will need to be specific about what it is you expect them to do. You cannot presume that they will understand your intentions unless you give them clear information – however skilled or experienced practitioners are, they are not mind readers!

Some activities you will be providing for the learners in your care may need to be adapted to ensure that all the children can participate. If you are planning a food tasting activity, for example, have you ensured that none of the children have an allergy or religious objection to any of the foods you are using? Rather than excluding the child, it would be good practice to make sure your resources are carefully selected to make the activity inclusive. This is not always as straightforward as it may seem as there are sometimes hidden pitfalls! For example, most jelly sweets contain gelatine which is an animal-based product, therefore not suitable for vegetarians and some religious groups – you need to check ingredients carefully when planning all food-based activities. You must also work within the policies of the setting – some settings may not allow children to have sweets of any kind as part of their healthy eating policy.

It is important that you are aware of the legal frameworks that exist to help children who have been identified as having a special educational need. Both the Special Education Needs Code of Practice (2001) – part of the Education Act (HMSO, 1996) – and the Special Educational Needs and Disability Act (HMSO, 2001) give guidance on meeting the needs of children who have been identified as having a need for provision,

> which is additional to, or otherwise different from, the educational provision made generally for children of their age in schools maintained by the LEA, other than special schools, in the area.
>
> (Section 312, HMSO, 1996)

There are now two additional categories to the SEN Code of Practice, that of Early Years Action (when extra resources need to be provided within the setting to help a child make progress in line with their peers) and Early Years Action Plus (when a setting cannot meet the needs of a child on their own and need to refer to an outside agency.) It is very important for you as a student to know if any child you are working with comes into either of these categories and what (if any) special programmes you might need to follow. It is vital that you know who to pass information on to if your observations or records are going to be used as part of an ongoing assessment procedure or profile. The information you have gathered may provide important details that will help to create a rounded picture of a child's progress or development.

There are many strategies that you can use that will be particularly beneficial for children who have additional learning needs, but will also be appropriate for all children.

- The use of multi-sensory resources and activities can be very effective, allowing children the opportunity to use touch, sight, hearing, taste and smell to experience the world.

- The use of sign language and visual symbols.

- Trips outside the setting to provide experience of the world in a practical way.

There are many resources and materials available for you to download from the EYFS Resources Index, which explores many of these issues in greater detail. One, an *Inclusion Checklist for Settings*, states that, *Inclusive practice is simply the core of all good practice* (Kids, 2005).

REFLECTIVE TASK

Think about your own attitudes to cultures or beliefs very different to your own. If you have a strong belief or faith, how easy is it for you to value one that may be very different? If you do not have a religious belief, how do you feel about people who do?

Keeping safe

There often seems to be confusion between issues of Health and Safety and Safeguarding. They both come under the ECM outcome of Staying Safe and although both will be dealt with in this chapter, there are some fundamental differences. The aim of good health and safety practice is to ensure that the environment is a safe place for babies and young children to be and that no practice carried out in the setting will put them at risk of serious injury or harm. It must also be recognised that the workplace must be a safe place for those working there and all settings must abide by Health and Safety legislation. Safeguarding is a relatively recently introduced term that is broader than child protection in that it also covers prevention. Safeguarding has been defined as:

The process of protecting children from abuse or neglect, preventing impairment of their health and development, and ensuring they are growing up in circumstances consistent with the provision of safe and effective care that enables children to have optimum life chances and enter adulthood successfully.

(HM Government, 2006)

This chapter will try to clarify some of the differences and will deal with health and safety issues first.

Health and safety

All toys and resources should be checked regularly to make sure they are in good repair and present no danger to the children. Many settings have environment checklists that have to be completed, perhaps for an outdoor area, prior to the children playing out. This would cover such things as checking for any litter that may have been thrown over a fence or wall – this might have specific information about what to do if you find a syringe for example, or it may be more general. Many settings also have bathroom area checklists to ensure that they are inspected regularly and kept clean and hygienic for the children to use. You may be asked to complete these checks, so it is essential that you understand why they are in place and how the setting expects them to be done.

Settings will have policies and procedures to follow when children are being dropped off and collected. Often they will be handed over to their Key Person and this may provide an opportunity for information to be shared. Some settings may allow students to be a part of this routine, but others feel it is more appropriate for the Key Person to retain the close relationship with parents and carers. Even if you are not actively encouraged to take an active part in this aspect of the daily routine, it will be valuable for you to observe how information is shared between the parent/carer and key worker. At the end of the day, when children are being picked up, there may be a chance for you to speak with parents or carers about activities or observations that you have done with the children during the day. If these opportunities do arise, it is a really good way of introducing yourself to parents and developing a relationship with them. It may be the case that students need to be flexible in their working patterns, to have the opportunity to meet parents and carers at each end of the day. In a school nursery setting, it is much more likely that you will see the parents at the beginning and end of each session, as the school day is often shorter than that of many day nurseries.

There are generally security procedures in place to make sure that only people with authorisation can enter the building. These can range from buzzers and intercoms to fingerprint recognition systems for parents and staff. There are also usually signing-in books to comply with fire regulations and visitors are often given badges to show that they have permission to be in the setting. You will probably have to show proof of identity when you first arrive and you should be prepared to provide the setting with your CRB number for their records. As a student, it may feel as though you are being excluded from certain routines for the children, but you have to be aware of how important these issues are for settings so they can ensure the safety of the children in their care.

You should be aware of the staff:child ratios that are specified in the EYFS Welfare Requirements, but as a student you should not be included in these ratios. Students are frequently asked to provide cover in different rooms to enable staff to take breaks or have their lunch and allow ratios to be maintained. This may give you the opportunity to gain experience of different age groups of children and babies, but if this is preventing you from doing placement tasks you should discuss this with your mentor or tutor.

New activities and trips outside the setting will have to have a risk assessment completed and as a student you may be asked to fill these in for activities that you plan. This can feel quite daunting at first, but your placement mentor should be able to help you with the paperwork. Every setting will have its own forms and a policy on risk assessment and you will need to become familiar with these. It is important to recognise that very few activities will be completely risk-free, but with careful thought and planning, risk can be minimised and potential dangers identified.

The Play Safety Forum, in its document *Managing Risk in Play Provision,* argues that:

> *In any human activity, there is an element of risk. Three factors are central to determining whether or not the level of risk is acceptable or tolerable:*
> * *The likelihood of coming to harm;*
> * *The severity of that harm;*
> * *The benefits, rewards or outcomes of the activity.*
> *Judgements about the acceptability of risk are made on the basis of a risk assessment. Risk assessment and management are not mechanistic processes. They crucially involve making judgements... based on an understanding of the balance between risks and benefits... Risks that are acceptable in one community may be unacceptable in another and policies should take this into account.*

(Play Safety Forum, 2002, page 2)

Babies and children have little sense of danger and so are vulnerable, but they need to learn about risk taking in a safe environment in order to develop these skills. If children never have the opportunity to take any risks, there is a chance that they will not learn how to recognise dangerous situations and will not be able to protect themselves from potential hazards. Part of keeping safe is learning about risk and every opportunity should be taken to discuss boundaries and why they are there. Children have a natural curiosity and they need to develop skills that will help them make good choices, assess risk and begin to keep themselves safe. Lindon (1999) suggests that if we want to protect children in the longer term, it is not sensible to keep them away from every risk. Dowling (2005) goes on to say that, *In one sense if we wrap children up in cotton wool we are not so much protecting them, but ourselves from taking the responsibility of helping them to understand what it means to grow up and be safety conscious.*

REFLECTIVE TASK

Think about your own attitudes to risk and danger. How might these differ from other practitioners and parents? What might be some of the potential conflicts caused by these attitudes and how might you begin to resolve these?

If a child has an accident while they are in the setting, this must be logged immediately and parents informed as soon as possible. If you have witnessed an incident, you must make sure your report is accurate and is written as soon as is practically possible after the event, certainly before you leave the setting for the day. Make sure you pass the information on verbally as well to the person who will hand the child over at the end of the day. If the incident involved any equipment, this must be reported and any risks further assessed.

PRACTICAL TASK

Read the examples of areas to be covered by risk assessments and the staff:child ratios in the Welfare Requirements section of the EYFS Practice Guidance. Makes notes about any particular aspects related to safe practice that you may encounter on your placement.

Safeguarding

It is vital that everyone who works with children has an understanding of safeguarding issues. It is imperative that you know who the designated person is within the setting who has responsibility for safeguarding. They may be called the safeguarding officer or the designated person and they will usually be a member of the Senior Management team. They have ultimate responsibility within a setting for liaison with other agencies. All settings must have a policy on safeguarding and this should be read as soon as possible when you begin a placement. There is a requirement for all practitioners to keep their knowledge of safeguarding up to date and these issues should be included in induction training. All staff should have access to regular training on safeguarding and how to promote the welfare of children.

There have been many well-documented cases of harm that has come to children where people had concerns about their welfare but failed to act to protect them; usually believing that 'someone else' would take action. Everyone has to take responsibility and acknowledge that safeguarding is an issue for all those who have contact with children, practitioners and students alike.

We all share responsibility for safeguarding and promoting the welfare of children and young people. All members of the community can help to safeguard and promote the

55

*welfare of children and young people if they are mindful of their needs, and willing
and able to act if they have concerns about a child's welfare.*

(HM Government, 2006)

It is important that we clarify exactly what we mean by safeguarding and what constitutes
child abuse. The National Society for the Prevention of Cruelty to Children (NSPCC) states
that there are five kinds of abuse:

- Physical abuse.

- Emotional abuse.

- Sexual abuse.

- Neglect.

- Bullying.   (NSPCC, 2006)

Until April 2008, children who were considered to be at risk of abuse were placed on a
local authority child protection register. These have now been phased out and replaced
with child protection plans, which are part of the Integrated Children's System (ICS).

Of the 25,900 children on child protection registers in England in 2005:

- 41% were under 4 years (10,400);

- 12% were under a year old (3,000). (Office for National Statistics, 2009)

These statistics show that many young children were believed to be at risk of serious harm
in 2005 and we have no reason to believe that the situation is particularly different today.

There may be particular difficulties in identifying when abuse may be happening to babies
and very young children because they do not have the language to express what is happening to them and there is often unwillingness on the part of practitioners to believe
that anyone could intentionally cause harm to such a vulnerable child. Everyone has
to accept that abuse does happen and that they have a duty to be vigilant in recognising it and raising concerns. The shocking 2009 case of child sexual abuse in a nursery in
Plymouth has highlighted the reality of the situation and many Early Years settings have
changed their policies to reflect these concerns. Many settings have made it a disciplinary
offence to be in possession of a mobile phone while on duty and cameras can only be
used when there is more than one person present. Again, you will have to check the policies of the setting you are placed in, to make sure you know what applies to you.

When practitioners get to know children really well, it becomes more apparent if they are
behaving in a way that is unusual for them. This can obviously be for many reasons, but
may indicate that the child is not happy about something that is happening in their lives.
You should be able to report and discuss anything that gives you a cause for concern;
other practitioners may have information that will put your mind at rest.

If a child arrives at a setting with an injury, parents or carers will be asked to complete a
form, documenting the wound and explaining how it happened. This not only provides
written documentation of any injury, but it is evidence that it did not happen while the
child was in the setting, preventing any future allegations against staff. This paperwork

may be particularly important if a child is dropped off by different people (perhaps a grandparent or childminder) and there are additional links in the chain of communication. It is easy for details to be forgotten and information overlooked unless it is written down. This evidence may also be useful if injuries happen frequently or if a pattern emerges and concerns need to be raised with an outside agency. If this paperwork has not been completed and you notice something, you should report it straightaway to an appropriate member of staff.

CHALLENGES and DILEMMAS

The NSPCC reports that practitioners often find it difficult to report or act on suspicions of child abuse. The main barriers or difficulties that people reported experiencing in deciding what to do about their concerns were the following:

- *Being unsure as to whether abuse was taking place.*
- *Being worried that if they did something it would have a negative impact on their relationship with the child's parents/carers.*
- *Thinking that it might make the situation worse for the child if they did something.*

(NSPCC, 2005)

CASE STUDY

Ellie is three and a half and has been attending the day nursery where you are a room leader since she was two. You are her Key Person and you feel you know her very well. You have a good relationship with her mum and don't feel too alarmed when Ellie arrives one morning with a large bruise on her cheek. Her mum tells you that she had a fall in the garden over the weekend while she was playing out. You log the injury and Mum is happy to sign the record. During the course of the day you notice that Ellie seems quiet and not her usual confident self, wanting lots of cuddles and staying near you. While playing with a doll in the afternoon, you see Ellie strike it with a hairbrush and shout 'naughty girl, don't touch mummy's make-up'. You feel that she might be acting out a situation and begin to feel uneasy.

Make some notes on the action you would take.

Health and well-being

In order for children to thrive, they must have all their needs met – both physically and emotionally. The EYFS states:

Being physically healthy is not simply about nutritious food. It also includes having a clean and safe environment; appropriate clothes; healthcare; mental stimulation; access to the outdoors and loving relationships.

(DCSF, 2008)

Children have an innate desire to move around and explore the world by using their physical senses. As they grow and develop their physical skills improve and they get better control over their whole bodies. This will only happen gradually and will happen at different rates for individual children. It will be dependent on a whole range of factors, both innate, for example a genetic medical condition (nature) and environmental experiences (nurture). We need to recognise that, as practitioners, we are responsible for considering all aspects of health and well-being. There are obvious links to other sections of this chapter (e.g. keeping safe and inclusive practice) but the subject also deserves further explicit consideration.

The EYFS Practice Guidance states that:

Early health provides a firm foundation for later life, whereas illness and deprivation cast long shadows forward. Children who enjoy good Health and Well-being are innately curious. They have a zest for life which results in their taking advantage of opportunities to grow and develop, to advance their knowledge, skills and attitudes in all areas of learning. They are strong, resilient and resourceful young people...

(DCSF, 2008)

Children who feel secure and valued and enjoy emotional well-being will be able to try things out and take risks. Pascal and Bertram (1998) have conducted a research project entitled 'Accounting Early for Life-Long Learning' in which they describe emotional well-being as one of the four factors seen in children who have potential to be effective learners. As a student, you will probably have to plan some physical activities, so these need to be appropriate for the children you are working with. All settings must have access to an outdoor environment, but the provision can vary tremendously. Some quite small spaces can be used very creatively to allow for a wide range of activities to take place while other potentially valuable environments are wasted.

PRACTICAL TASK

Find out how the outdoor provision is organised in your placement setting. Can children choose when to go outside, is it always available to them or are there more formal 'going out' times? What are the factors that influence this?

If the children cannot go outside frequently, what physical activities are on offer indoors?

Most settings will operate a healthy eating policy, providing milk or water and fruit at snack time instead of sugary biscuits and drinks. A British Medical Association survey in 1999, found that many children and babies in the lowest income group had inadequate diets that did not contain the full range of vitamins and minerals. These families are now entitled to receive Healthy Start vouchers that they can exchange for free milk or fresh fruit and vegetables to encourage better eating habits. Where a setting provides meals on the premises, these should be nutritious and well-balanced. It is much more difficult to ensure that where children bring packed lunches, these are also healthy. Settings can give advice to parents, but it is impossible to insist on the contents of a lunch box. Some settings have looked at the topic of food and encouraged children to learn about foods that are good for them. This might be a subject that you, as a student, might be able to address as a possible area for change, if this is appropriate.

As previously discussed, you need to note any allergies that the children may have and ensure that the child is not given any potentially harmful foods. A useful strategy is for each child to have a laminated place mat with their picture and name on one side and a list of any foods they need to avoid on the other. This ensures that any agency staff or students, who may not be familiar with all the children, do not accidentally offer a dangerous foodstuff. Some foods are potentially fatal so this must be taken very seriously.

The EYFS (DCSF, 2008) states that, *Brain development depends on nourishment: a good diet, in both the form of food and of physical and psychological stimulation.*

Children do enjoy eating food that they have grown themselves and, even with very limited space, there can be opportunities to plant and grow vegetables and some fruit in containers. Salad leaves grow quite fast so the children do not have to wait too long for results and strawberries and tomatoes usually yield quite a good crop. Herbs provide a wonderful multi-sensory experience for the children. These planting activities provide the opportunity for speaking and listening and possibly sustained, shared thinking.

Hygiene routines are important and children quickly learn why they need to wash their hands after the toilet and before touching food. It is also important that you observe any practices like wearing gloves when changing nappies or cleaning children who have been ill. Many settings have visits from health professionals such as a Community Dentist who will talk to the children about looking after their teeth and will often provide resources for health topics. This again is something that you might be able to organise if this is not already in place.

It is part of your role to promote the ECM outcome Stay Healthy, and support children in making healthy choices. This may be a challenge when the home environment does not support healthy choices and you will need to be sensitive to children's experiences – promoting possibly unfamiliar routines or experiences without being negative about their parents' decisions or lifestyles. It is also vital that babies and children are cared for by someone who is special to them to enable them to feel valued and develop a sense of self-worth. They need to develop secure attachments in order to thrive emotionally as well as physically. These attachments will also help them develop the resilience they will need in order to bounce back from life's adversities. (This is dealt with in much greater detail in Chapter 5.) Although the key person role is pivotal, all the adults in a setting, including students, need to show kindness, respect and genuine regard for the children. There are times during the day when sensitive issues can be discussed through the use of stories or circle time activities. This would usually be an opportunity for a key worker to sit with their key group, but students sometimes have the chance to take part in these sessions. As well as being a positive role model for staff, as previously mentioned, it is important that you are a good role model for the children, demonstrating the behaviours and attitudes you wish to see from them. Children learn from everyone around them so you need to show that you are kind, caring, calm (when necessary), but also enthusiastic and able to have fun!

REFLECTIVE TASK

Read some articles or books about circle time activities and how they can help children's emotional development. Consider the value of circle time, and the key features of the approach. Also consider, conversely, what the possible issues may be when it is used as a 'quick fix' solution to playground conflicts. There are some suggestions for further reading at the end of the chapter.

C H A P T E R   S U M M A R Y

Every child is unique with individual needs and interests. They have an entitlement to have these needs addressed by practitioners who understand the principles and philosophy of inclusive practice. Practitioners need to have an understanding of health and safety issues and be able to promote safeguarding principles.

REFERENCES

Abbot, L and Langston, A (2005) *Birth to Three Matters. Supporting the Framework of Effective Practice*. Maidenhead: OUP.

Baldock, P (2010) *Understanding Cultural Diversity in the Early Years*. London: Sage.

DCSF (2008) *Practice Guidance for the Early Years Foundation Stage*. London: DCSF.

DCSF (2008) *Statutory Framework for the Early Years Foundation Stage*. London: DCSF.

DfEE (1996) SEN Code of Practice. London: HMSO.

DfES (2002) *Birth to Three Matters*. London: DfES Publications.

Dowling, M (2005) *Young Children's Personal, Social and Emotional Development* (2nd ed). London: Paul Chapman.

HM Government (1996) Education Act. London: HMSO.

HM Government (2001) Special Education Needs and Disability Act.London: HMSO.

HM Government (2006) Working Together to Safeguard Children. London: HMSO.

Katz, LG (1991) Pedagogical Issues in Early Childhood Education, in Kagan, SL (ed.) *The Care and Education of America's Young Children: Obsatcles and Opportunities. Ninetieth Yearbook of the National Society for the Study of Education. Part I*. Chicago: University of Chicago Press.

Lindon, J (1999) *Too Safe for their Own Good*. London: National Early Years Network.

NSPCC www.NSPCC.org.uk

Nutbrown, C (2006) *Threads of Thinking* (3rd ed). London: Sage.

Office for National Statistics www.statistics.gov.uk

Pascal, C and Bertram, T (1998) Accounting for Lifelong Learning. Keynote speech at Early Years Conference, Dorchester.

Play Safety Forum (2002) *Managing Risk in Play Provision*. Play Safety Forum.

Read, V (2010) *Developing Attachments in Early Years Settings*. London: Routledge.

Siraj-Blatchford, I (2001) Diversity and Learning in the Early Years, in Pugh, G (2001) *Contemporary Issues in the Early Years: Working Collaboratively*. London: Sage.

Smidt, S (2006) *The Developing Child in the 21st Century, A Global Perspective on Child Development*. London: Routledge.

Sylva, K and Siraj-Blatchford I (1996) *Bridging the Gap between Home and School,* Improving achievment in Primary Schools. Paris: Unesco.

FURTHER READING

Cairns, K (2002) *Attachment, Trauma and Resilience, Therapeutic Caring for Children*. London: BAAF.

Mosley, J (2005) *The Circle Book (Circle Time)*. Wiltshire: Positive Press.

Pugh, G and Duffy, B (2006) *Contemporary Issues in the Early Years* (4th ed). London: Sage.

Selleck, D (2006) Key Persons in the Early Years Foundation Stage, *Early Education,* Autumn.

5 Positive relationships

Wendy Whittaker

CHAPTER OBJECTIVES

By the end of this chapter you should understand:

- *how your ability to be emotionally intelligent affects areas of your work;*
- *why developing positive relationships with other professionals is crucial;*
- *how you can deepen your relationship with parents;*
- *how to help children develop friendships;*
- *how attachment provides a basis for a child's ability to form secure and fulfilling relationships;*
- *why the key person role is so important for children and parents;*
- *why listening to children takes time and energy if it is to be effective.*

This chapter addresses the following Professional Standards for QTS and EYPS:
QTS: Q1; 2; 4; 5; 6; 32; 33.
EYPS: S6; 14; 22; 23; 25; 26; 27; 28; 29; 30; 31; 32; 33; 34; 35; 36.

Introduction

> *Children learn to be strong and independent from a base of loving and secure relationships with parents and/or a key person.*
>
> (DCSF, 2008)

For children to flourish, they need to be nurtured emotionally. Creating, developing and maintaining positive relationships is literally at the heart of effective practice in Early Years. The EYFS acknowledges the importance that positive relationships play in the lives of children and adults by making this a core theme within the framework, and it is worthwhile reflecting and trying to expand on what is said in the EYFS to deepen your knowledge and application of why relationships are so important to high quality Early Years practice.

Your role can be described in many ways – as a guide, caregiver, co-learner, pedagogue – but however you describe it, working with and caring for young children requires you to be emotionally mature, sensitive, responsive, warm and to be able to manage your own relationships well. By developing knowledge and insight about your own skills and competencies in managing relationships, you will understand how you can support children to do the same.

A child's learning is built on a foundation of emotions, which, as their teacher, you make a significant contribution towards. For children who need extra support due to poverty, additional needs, language barriers or other reasons, your role is vital in ensuring that they develop emotional resilience to cope with their life circumstances. The importance of emotional stability cannot be overestimated in terms of the contribution it makes towards a child's ability to learn effectively. This chapter will help you analyse some strategies to support children who may need extra help, and reflect on which might create the most positive impact.

There may be areas of your own personal development which you have identified as being strong in building relationships, but equally there may be areas you have struggled with – such as working with parents, or other professionals. These are areas which are explored in this chapter and which will help you to think about the wider context of children's lives.

Positive relationships within the EYFS

The EYFS breaks down the Positive Relationships principle into a number of commitments. By understanding the theory that underpins each concept and by reflecting on your own attitudes and practice, you will gain insight that will help you develop more fulfilling, healthy relationships with children and families in your setting. It will help you make the necessary changes and work towards developing improved skills and attitudes. Each of the commitments works as a puzzle piece, and when fitted together they create a spectrum of advice and information to stretch Early Years practitioners and support settings. Each one is designed to support you develop personally and professionally and is based on a wide body of research and evidence that tells us how children learn and develop most effectively.

2.1 Respecting each other

Understanding and recognising feelings
The recognition that feelings form the basis for many of our relationships is espoused by Daniel Goleman in his book, *Emotional Intelligence*, where he states that *our deepest feelings, our passions and longings, are essential guides, and [that] our species owes much of its existence to their power in human affairs* (1996, page 4). Much of how we behave and react is based on deep-seated emotional responses. These are ones that we have learnt or instinctively developed from birth. The ability to recognise, identify and understand our feelings is crucial if we are to form relationships that are real and reciprocal.

Anyone who has experienced a time when their own emotions were overpowering and when they needed support from others to function because of these feelings will know how emotions can become supreme and can affect our ability to eat, sleep and think. Our ability to manage and identify our emotions is the first aspect of being able to build effective and fulfilling relationships. Relationships are dynamic; ever-changing as a result of events, personal development, and interactions. Emotions guide and shape these dynamic changes and act as a kind of currency in the emotional 'bank account' (Covey, 1989). They build trust, empathy, security and belief, and when built on, these aspects are what maintain and build a relationship. Sometimes, emotions cause us to behave in seemingly irrational or bizarre ways, and this may be because they are set within our unconscious, and we have not yet become fully conscious of them, which creates a blockage in our ability to cope with them. Being aware of our emotions is the first step in being able to manage them. As Goleman asserts: *Emotions that simmer beneath the threshold of awareness can have a powerful impact on how we perceive and react, even though we have no idea they are at work* (1996, page 55).

We communicate our feelings in a number of ways, including tone of voice, body language (or non-verbal communication) and content of speech. Your non-verbal communication will tell others more than you might realise about how you feel. You need to develop an awareness of how you communicate non-verbally. Try the following self-analysis to consider how emotionally intelligent you are, and whether there are areas that you need to develop further.

Consider the following statements and mark down your responses.

	yes	no
When having a conversation with someone, are you able to concentrate on the person you are talking to and feel 'connected' to them?		
Are you comfortable with pauses? Do you feel at ease when no one is speaking?		
Do you sense when someone feels troubled before being told?		
Are you critical of yourself feeling certain emotions?		
Do you pay attention to your gut feelings when making important decisions?		
Are you able to identify when you become stressed?		
Do you know how to quickly calm yourself down when you're stressed?		
Are you able to tease others and make fun of yourself?		
Can you use humour to overcome tricky issues?		

Table 5.1 Test your emotional intelligence

Supporting children in developing friendships

Helping children to manage their feelings and develop an ability to form lasting relationships should start from birth. Trevarthen (2001) has demonstrated how very young babies indicate emotion through facial expression, gesture and vocalisations. Just as young infants react to others and attempt to build relationships and understand others through the indicators of emotional response, children and adults too cannot help but communicate their emotions through facial expression, body language and speech. As a practitioner, your job is to be able to interpret these signals in young children who may not be able to tell you what they feel at any given time. By being sensitive and responsive, practitioners can identify emotions in a child from the first time they start to care for them, and over time help the child to recognise and 'label' the emotion.

Young babies and children have not yet developed the capability of regulating their own emotions so therefore require high levels of sensitivity and response from their caregivers to learn how to do this. In fact, how a child ultimately learns how to regulate their emotions will depend heavily on how the caregiver(s) regulates their own emotions. As children become better at expressing their needs and emotions, they learn self-regulation skills. However, this 'dyadic' (two-way) regulation never entirely disappears (Sroufe, 1995). One of the keys to understanding children's emotions is through emotional 'attunement' (Stern, 1985). This requires high levels of sensitivity as you watch, interact with and respond to children. You need to be sensitive to the verbal and non-verbal cues of the child so that you can feel what they feel, and in essence, put yourself into the mind of that child.

Children need to develop social skills to allow them to interact effectively and congenially with one another; to make their own needs known and to help meet the needs of others. Your role as key person is of considerable importance as you provide the underpinning emotional stability that a child needs to build reciprocal friendships.

Children who are shy or find it difficult to co-operate with others may find it particularly difficult to make friends. A child on the autistic spectrum may find it impossible to consider other children's feelings. Occasionally situations arise where one child has a seemingly dominant role in a friendship, which tends to overshadow the personality of another child. These types of behaviour can cause friction for children and worry for parents and adults. It is important that you do not quickly jump to conclusions about children who exhibit behaviours which test friendships in the setting. There may be other reasons than the interplay between one child and another that is affecting their behaviour such as: a situation at home, tiredness, feeling accepted, or lack of confidence. Not only do you need to model friendly behaviour, but you need to spend time with children who find friendships problematic, talking about how to respond appropriately, and helping them to understand how others feel in certain situations.

Practical suggestions for helping create a positive social environment include:

- ensuring that there are sufficient resources for children who like playing with the same resource (such as sand or bricks) to avoid potential conflicts;

- making the book corner welcoming and sociable, with plenty of soft cushions, beanbags and sofas to allow interaction and sharing;

- using books to talk about the feelings of the characters and the reasons they might feel a certain way;

- recognising that where children have similar interests they may develop stronger friendships;

- bringing children to play together who do not normally do so;

- spending time at, for example, mealtimes and snack time talking about food children like and using simple opportunities to help children realise others have different preferences;

- using 'Persona Dolls' to exemplify and explore emotions and to help children learn to recognise uncomfortable feelings as well as good ones;

- developing strong relationships through the key person system to prevent problems developing.

Ultimately, though, it is your reflective response as key person to a child that will set the tone for the room or setting. If you determine to respond calmly, positively, sensitively and warmly you will be able to deal with a child who may find friendships easy or hard.

Setting an example through open and friendly professional relationships

In an ideal world, your workplace relationships would run smoothly and create a sense of shared collaborative purpose that would be mutually fulfilling. However, it is very likely that in your setting you will have to work with people who you do not find easy. There may be all sorts of reasons for this, including differences in values and expectations, different perceptions of the role or task, differences in how you communicate, or differences in personality. Working in multi-professional settings, such as Children's Centres, there are many professional disciplines represented, and the perceptions about children and families may well be different from yours. Creating open and professional relationships is crucial to you in your work, to ensure that children's needs are met effectively. In order to achieve the best outcomes for children, professionals have to respect and value others' input, whatever role or position they hold, and this is true whether or not a child needs specialised intervention. If a child is in need of additional support, this may be organised through a Common Assessment Framework (CAF). There will be a named lead professional who will co-ordinate the input from other professionals and work closely with the family to ensure their views are heard and their consent is upheld.

The following factors are core to developing strong professional relationships:

- Being able to resolve conflict.

- Forging trusting relationships.

- Building expectations that create optimistic yet realistic goals.

- Creating rapport and a sense of conviviality and team spirit.

- Listening to the feelings of others and responding to them appropriately.

- Communicating wisely; neither being too forceful or timid.

Often it is a personal or emotional connection at a social level that strengthens relationships the most, and giving time to get to know one another aside from your professional role is essential. Quality relationships on a professional level allow individuals to express themselves, develop their role, and receive support from others while maintaining their professionalism.

CHALLENGES and DILEMMAS

Liz is a newly qualified EYP who has just started work at Cranbrook Children's Centre. There is a large team of staff, representing a number of disciplines, including Roger who is a health visitor. At a recent team meeting, the Children's Centre manager asked for suggestions about how they might spend an additional small pot of money they had been given to develop services for teenage parents. Liz made a couple of suggestions, based on her conversations with teenage parents of children who were accessing the nursery on a part-time basis.

The next day, Liz was in the staffroom, when Roger came in and coolly stated to her: 'You don't know what you're talking about regarding teenage parents; I've worked in the area for twenty years and think I have a better understanding than you. They don't need education, they need social opportunities.' *After which he walked out of the staffroom.*

Later on, Liz overheard Roger 'rubbishing' her idea to the Children's Centre manager, stating 'she has little experience and is just trying to impress you'. *Liz felt very upset by what she heard as she felt undermined and undervalued.*

- *What skills does Liz need to be able to deal with this situation effectively?*
- *What might be her continuing course of action?*
- *How would you address the situation?*

2.2 Parents as partners

Respecting diversity by valuing all families

> *When each person is valued for who they are and differences are appreciated, everyone feels included and understood, whatever their personality, abilities, ethnic background or culture.*

(EYFS, 2008)

For a child growing up in Britain today, their experience of family life, Early Years services and community culture is very different from 20 or 30 years ago. We live in a vastly more complex society where people from many backgrounds, beliefs, values and languages live and work together. A child's own learning about the world will be shaped and influenced by these alternatives. Political, environmental, technical and social changes also have a huge impact on a child's experiences of growing up. In terms of changes to Early Years care and education, Children's Centres have emerged as being central to provision, particularly in a multi-professional context, and they have had a significant impact on the shape of services today. Therefore, as an Early Years practitioner you need to be aware of these various strands of influence on a young child, and how the children you nurture are affected by the communities they grow up in – remembering that your setting is but one part of that eclectic mix.

Your own background and culture will influence your approach to working with families, even if subtly and unintentionally. Recognising your own influences and beliefs and reflecting on these influences will help you clarify what your own values are and how you might come across some unexpected difficulties when working with families from a variety of backgrounds. Respecting diversity is a hugely important aspect of Early Years, as it indicates to families and children their worth in your eyes. By failing to value diversity you are communicating to families that their cultural context is insignificant and has no contribution to make to their child's learning. Bronfenbrenner's theory of ecological development (1979) indicates that the various interconnected layers of a child's cultural and daily context has a huge impact on their learning and identity. Your setting will play a considerable role in defining a child's perspective on the value of their own identity. The value and understanding you place on their home background, and the importance it plays in the child's life, will enable you to deepen the child's learning far more effectively. This also opens the door to a closer relationship with parents and carers as they recognise your willingness to appreciate their strengths rather than personifying a didactic, 'we know best' approach. Involving them directly (such as inviting parents and children to actively help you plan and make decisions about the way the setting is run), and embedding these values in the operational aspects of your provision (such as through reflecting children's home language in the setting), will assist in making everyone who uses the setting feel valued.

Good and welcoming communication by approachable staff

As has already been discussed, regular, effective two-way communication between parents and staff is vital for a child's well-being and learning. How you behave really sets the tone for the interaction with parents and children – remember what has been said earlier about non-verbal communication. Parents may need to express how they feel and to be supported to express difficult emotions, such as worry, fear and frustration. The start of the day and when children are being collected, marks one of the transitions of the child's day so particular importance needs to be paid to ensuring the key person (or his/her back-up) is available to communicate with families and be a familiar face for the child. Throughout the day parents need to feel that they can contact the setting with any concerns or practical information that needs to be conveyed. It may be necessary for staff to have additional training on telephone skills or customer care so that they do not become the cause of anxiety for parents who feel that their concerns are not treated as being important.

Learning together with parents

When settings embrace parents and carers as co-learners on their learning journey, a much deeper dialogue becomes possible about the child. The REPEY (Siraj-Blatchford et al., 2002) research emphatically demonstrated that children do better in settings where practitioners share a pedagogical approach with parents, and where this happens most effectively is where the curriculum is jointly shared. EPPE (Sylva et al., 2004) research demonstrated that one of the factors that created a high quality setting was encouraging mutual learning by parents, staff and children as they shared observations and insights together. This is likely to strengthen the quality of the home learning environment, which EPPE concluded was

> *more important for intellectual and social development than parental occupation, education or income. What parents do is more important than who parents are.*

(Sylva et al., 2004, page ii)

When parents and practitioners share observations, and insights, and learn together, they can plan and provide appropriate resources, experiences and learning opportunities that really reflect the intrinsic motivation of the child. In addition, there are a number of added benefits for each partner when it comes to assessing a child's learning. These are:

- *that parents can describe their children fully and 'accurately';*
- *parental information and perspectives complement professional assessment and perspectives;*
- *assessment partners share concerns, report upon progress/problems, jointly celebrate success, use assessment data to monitor progress, plan next steps;*
- *each partner gains important knowledge of the child in other settings.*

(Wolfendale, 2004, page 5)

A true partnership with parents recognises the strengths and contribution that parents make to their child's welfare. The attitude and activity of staff in the setting will display most notably how importantly they view the role of parents. You may have a parental involvement policy, but it will be your attitude to developing learning in partnership with parents that will personify a far more enticing invitation.

PRACTICAL TASK

Starting at the front entrance, take a walk around your setting, and note how it communicates to parents. (Think about messages you might convey without meaning to!)

- *Are there some messages that express 'you're not welcome'? (Such as an empty front desk, an off-putting sign, or a plethora of rules?)*
- *What barriers to parents are there? (Physical, linguistic, cultural, institutional.)*
- *Are there some messages that need to be changed to be more parent-friendly?*

2.3 Supporting learning

Of all the factors that affect the capacity for learning, the capacity for relationship is considered to be critical (Malaguzzi, 1993, cited in Rodd, 1999).

Promoting positive interactions with all children and families

As you deepen your knowledge about the children in your care you will begin to understand their specific strengths, developmental achievements, abilities and preferences. You will also begin to understand more about their family and the context of the child's life, of which you see only a slice. These influences will subtly influence their learning, which is why it is so important not only to know about them but to relate them to your practice.

Young children learn from a basis of relationships, and these relationships are built on the small, shared individual transactions of everyday life. As a practitioner working with young children you need to see yourself engaged on a learning journey with the children with whom you work. Children need adults to explore the world with them, and your journey of discovery should be focused on understanding the children themselves; what interests and motivates them, and how to stimulate and inspire their exploratory drive. This journey is filled with positive experiences, laughter, fun and humour. It revels in apparent dead ends, where problems can be solved, and it celebrates creativity. It is a journey where time is taken to enjoy each other's company and where affection is felt amicably and authentically. This is what forms the basis of positive interactions.

The EYFS states that effective practitioners work in the following ways.

- *They build respectful and caring relationships with all children and families while focusing on learning and achievement.*
- *They observe children sensitively and respond appropriately to encourage and extend curiosity and learning.*
- *By observing and listening they discover what children like to do, and when they feel confident, scared or frustrated.*
- *They are able to tune in to, rather than talk at, children, taking their lead and direction from what the children say or do.*

(EYFS, 2008)

Tuning into children happens in a variety of ways, but one of the most powerful ways is through observations. Further reference is made to this in Chapter 6.

Listening to children
In *The Mosaic Approach* (2001) Clark and Moss suggest a 'framework' for listening to children which is:

- multi-method: recognises the different languages or voices of children;
- participatory: treats children as experts and agents in their own lives;
- reflexive: includes children, practitioners and parents in reflecting on meanings and addresses the question of interpretation;
- adaptable: can be applied to a variety of early childhood institutions;
- focused on children's lived experiences: looking at lives rather than knowledge gained or care received;
- embedded into practice: a framework for listening which has the potential to be both used as an evaluative tool and to become embedded into Early Years practice.

(Clark and Moss, 2001)

It is important to recognise that children are highly emotionally sensitive, and though they might not be able to communicate their emotions through verbal communication, they will communicate through non-verbal means and behaviour.

Effective teaching
In Early Years, practitioners need to have particular skills to identify the learning that children are experiencing. They need to be observant and perceptive, but also creative,

reflective and have high expectations. They need to be resourceful and playful and be able to place themselves at the child's level as if to see the world through the child's eyes. They need to be prepared to seek for answers persistently and to hypothesise about what children might be learning, in order to provide potential possibilities in their planning and resourcing. Young children need to learn certain essentials, there is no doubting that, but *how* they learn these essentials is what effective teaching encompasses.

Adopting an appropriate pedagogy is crucial if a child's thinking skills are to be challenged, stretched and stimulated. In Early Years we need to articulate our pedagogy for, as Athey asserts: *a teacher's pedagogy permeates his or her thinking on practically every educational issue, from the more general to the more specific* (2007, page 38). (Chapter 7 deals with teaching and learning in more detail.)

2.4 Key person

Secure attachment
The main theory that underpins the key person approach is attachment theory, which helps explain how people learn to regulate emotion, develop strong relationships, and express confident, capable selves. John Bowlby (1982/1969) used the term *attachment* to describe the affective bond that develops between an infant and a primary caregiver. He believed that the *attachment behavioural system* was part of a necessary human drive to ensure survival of the species. To develop a secure attachment with a caregiver, a child needs to have:

- a carer who can 'tune into' the child;
- his/her distress responded to quickly and promptly;
- moderate stimulation;
- sensitive intervention;
- an emotionally warm relationship;
- involvement and interest from the adult;
- an adult who responds appropriately and consistently.

(based on Fonagy, 1997)

In Early Years practice, there has been a rapidly growing emphasis placed on attachment and its role in creating confident, fulfilled children, partly due to a plethora of research which has demonstrated the importance of a secure emotional base for learning. According to EPPE research (2004), one of the notable markers that sets quality provision apart is the quality of relationships within that setting – indeed, guidance for the EYFS states: *what matters most in 'achieving quality' is carers who are 'attentive, responsive, stimulating and affectionate'* (Effective Practice: Key Person, DCSF, 2008, page 2).

June has worked at ABC day nursery in the toddler room for over five years, and she has always been able to develop close relationships with the children in her room, along with the other staff. Since the EYFS was introduced, the nursery has moved to a key person system, and she is nominally key person to four of the toddlers in her room. However, if she is honest, she doesn't really know what this means, and hasn't been given clear guidance from her manager. She also has worries about the practicalities of running a key person system in a busy day nursery, when she really believes that all children should develop a relationship with all the staff. She can see in theory some of the positive aspects of being a key person, but she has questions about how practical it is in a toddler room:

- *How should we run the key person system when one of us has a day off or is ill?*
- *If I am off, does this negatively affect my key children?*
- *All the staff share nappy changing and organising mealtimes – is this appropriate?*
- *How can I develop a better relationship with the parents when there's so little time to talk?*
- *Shouldn't children learn to develop relationships with lots of different people, otherwise they risk becoming clingy?*

What advice would you give June about developing a less superficial key person approach? What practical advice could you give her? How could you encourage her to persevere with the key person approach?

Early Years practitioners need to be emotionally intelligent. You need to have the capacity to hear the distress of a child: *their dependency and their inherent mess and chaos* (Manning-Morton and Thorp 2006, page 6) and respond appropriately, in an emotionally warm way – yet continue to view the child as a powerful active learner. This is, however, a hard task! You may need the support of a supervisor or manager to assist you in reflecting on your role as key person and working through some of the sensitivities that may arise as a result. Support for you as practitioner in enabling you to be an effective key person comes further in the form of shared care.

Shared care
The principle of shared care described in the EYFS espouses the ideal triangulation of relationships between the child's primary caregiver (normally his/her parents), the child him/herself, and the key person in the setting. The key person's supervisor and the setting itself are also part of the backdrop of shared care. For shared care to work effectively, adults need to make time to develop an understanding of each other, and to understand their relationship with the child. The key person needs to make it a priority to ensure that parents or carers are valued and that this relationship should be a priority. By working in this way, the parents and the setting's staff are supported to provide the best environment for the child. This is fundamentally important for a number of reasons:

- Support and continuity for the child – when his/her primary caregiver and key person share information, ideas, thoughts and reflections about the child's learning and well-being, this strengthens the network of knowledge about the child.

- Emotional support for the adults – allowing for opportunities to share concerns, hopes, fears and anxieties, knowing that another person understands the context of those concerns.

- Practical back-up and reduction of risk – practitioners are able to understand the context of the child's life and provide signposts to additional services and support for parents, while parents are more likely to disclose information knowing that there is support, not judgement, waiting for them.

- Professional support and accountability – parents and practitioners feel more confident to share concerns within a context of trust and confidentiality, knowing that there are policies and processes in place to keep the child at the centre of care.

You may have children in your setting who are also cared for by a childminder some parts of the week, and perhaps also attend a before- or after-school club. Dorothy Selleck (2006) called this 'serial care', where children move from setting to setting throughout the week, with little regard to the impact that such numerous transitions have on the child. These multifarious transitions can place stress upon a child, which *demands adjustment and brings about changes in identity, relations and roles* (Nielsen and Griebel, 2008, page 23). Transition has an impact on the whole family and wider environment that the child inhabits.

CASE STUDY

Jim and Marie have been together for five years, and they have a four-year-old daughter called Susanna. Jim has two sons from his previous marriage who stay at their house at the weekend. The boys often stay over on Sunday nights.

On Monday morning, Jim leaves the house early to get to work, and drops his boys off at their mum's house on the way. Marie and Susanna have to get up early on Monday mornings so that Marie can get everything ready for Susanna and get to work on time. She doesn't have a car, so they have to walk across town to get to the childminder's house by 8 a.m. At 8.40 a.m. the childminder takes Marie to her nursery.

Questions to think about:

- *What transitions is Susanna coping with on a Monday morning?*
- *What impact might all these arrangements have on Marie and Jim?*
- *What might Susanna feel as a result?*
- *How could she be supported through these transitions?*

For many settings, shared care is an aspect of practice that needs constant assessment and reflection. It requires staff to be emotionally mature themselves, and to understand the tensions and stresses of parenthood, and the many competing demands made on parents. It also requires a commitment from staff to create an emotionally enabling environment for parents and children – so that parents can talk about issues or concerns knowing they will not be judged or gossiped about once they have left the room.

For parents who see day care as a service to enable their child to be safely cared for while they are at work, they may initially resist or question the need for such an open relationship with professionals who in their eyes are paid to care for their child. You need to demonstrate the importance of mutuality and respect, where your professional knowledge is underpinned by professional behaviour, which firstly listens to parents and carers, and seeks to understand their position, before moving forward to develop the relationship at a deeper level. With some parents, this takes a great deal of effort and time. You will need to address the practicalities of this occurring in, for example, a busy Reception class, where you only see parents for a few minutes each day in the playground. Together with the manager or head, you might want to consider the following questions and reflect on the changes you need to make:

- Does our setting allow parents and carers to come in whenever they wish?

- Does our setting provide a room or space for parents to meet one another, or relax?

- How many ways do we encourage communication between key person and parent?

- How can we help deepen that relationship?

- What can we do to listen more to parental concerns and respond to them?

- How closely do we work with other settings who regularly care for this child?

- How can we ensure that vertical transitions (within the setting) create as little stress as possible?

In addition, it is vitally important that staff have a regular opportunity to share their thoughts, concerns or insights about their key person role with another person in the setting, who acts in a supervisory capacity. Within an environment of confidentiality, there need to be conversations that allow the key person to express their own feelings and reflections on the relationship, and receive support and input from their supervisor.

Independence

Children have a natural curiosity and desire to explore which is clearly observable from birth. Although children have an innate physiological capacity for learning, this can be stilted through lack of an appropriately stimulating and supporting environment, and from children not having the emotional courage to explore. This may be as a result of anxiety, illness, low levels of confidence or insecurity, which is why the adult role is so important. Becoming independent means that a child develops the capacity to solve problems autonomously and assertively – it does not mean that they no longer need other people (peers and adults) to engage with them in their play.

The adult role is especially important at this age, as children need regular reassurance and support to feel the rewards from exploration, in what may be extremely new and unfamiliar territory. You should not be surprised if you need to support a child's independence by:

- accepting their dependent behaviour;

- protecting them from distress and the unfamiliar;

- helping them to explore the unfamiliar;

- explaining and showing new experiences or resources;

- introducing small novel experiences;

- holding the child physically and supporting them emotionally;

- using language, tone of voice and body language to communicate security.

(Elfer et al., DCSF, 2008)

REFLECTIVE TASK

Consider a young boy who has come to your setting and cannot speak English, who may have been cared for by his grandmother in a home where there is little opportunity for outdoor play. The food, language, routine and culture are completely different from those at nursery. His need for reassurance, warmth and support will be much greater than another child who is familiar with the setting, and knows the culture of the setting.

- *What kind of behaviour might be demonstrated by the child?*
- *What activities might be inappropriate for this child?*
- *What could you do to encourage the child's independence and emotional courage?*

C H A P T E R   S U M M A R Y

As an Early Years practitioner, you have a unique opportunity to impact the lives of many children by instilling positive values, encouraging emotional resilience and inspiring constructive dispositions to learn. The foundations of positive relationships that you build with the children in your care will influence their lives consciously and unconsciously. Your role as key person is critical to a child's emotional resilience and security, and by developing this as an effective three-way system with the child's parents and carers you can create a triad of support. In reading this chapter you may have been struck by some areas of practice that are unfamiliar to you. The theme of Positive Relationships is centrally important to the EYFS as a foundation for effective learning in a child's life, and you can be a part of that process as you take on and connect with the ideas and challenges presented in this section.

REFERENCES

Athey, C (2007) *Extending Thought in Young Children* (2nd ed.). London: Paul Chapman.

Bowlby, J (1969) *Attachment*. New York: Basic Books.

Bronfenbrenner, U (1979) *The Ecology of Human Development: Experiments by Nature and Design*. Cambridge, MA: Harvard University Press.

Carr, M and Claxton, G *(2002)* Tracking the Development of Learning Dispositions. *Assessment in Education,* Vol. 9 (1): 9–37.

Covey, S (1989) *Seven Habits of Highly Effective People*. London: Simon & Schuster.

Fonagy (1997) Attachment, the Development of the Self, and its Pathology in Personality Disorders, in Dervison, Maffei and Greon, *Treatment of Personality Disorders*. New York: Kluwer Academic/ Plenum Publishers.

Goleman, D (1996) *Emotional Intelligence*. London: Bloomsbury.

Gopnik, A, Meltzoff, A and Kuhl, P (1999) *How Babies Think: the Science of Childhood*. London: Weidenfeld and Nicolson.

Grenier, J, Manning-Morton, J and Elfer, P (2008) Babies, Young Children and their Key Adults: Relationships to Support Thinking. *Early Childhood Forum*. ppt

Manning-Morton, J and Thorp, M (2006) *Key Times: A Framework for Developing High Quality Provision for Children From Birth to Three*. Maidenhead: Open University Press.

Nielsen and Griebel (2008) Enhancing the Competence of Transition Systems Through Co-construction, in Dunlop, A-W and Fabian, H (2008) *Informing Transitions in the Early Years*. Maidenhead: Open University Press.

Rodd, G (1999) Encouraging Young Children's Critical and Creative Thinking Skills: an Approach in one English Elementary School. *Childhood Education* 75(6): 350–54.

Selleck, D (2006) Key Persons in the Early Years Foundation Stage. *Early Education*, Autumn.

Sroufe, A (1995) *Emotional Development: The Organization of Emotional Life in the Early Years*. New York: Cambridge University Press.

Stern, D (1985). *The Interpersonal World of the Infant: A View From Psychoanalysis and Developmental Psychology.* New York: Basic.

Sylva, K, Melhuish, E, Sammons, P, Siraj-Blatchford, I and Taggart, B (2004) *Effective Provision of Preschool Education (EPPE) Project*. Final Report. London: DfES.

Trevarthen, C (2001) Intrinsic Motives for Companionship in Understanding: Their Origin, Development and Significance for Infant Mental Health. *International Journal of Infant Mental Health*, 22(1–2): 95–131.

Wolfendale, S (2004) *Getting the Balance Right: Towards Partnership in Assessing Children's Development and Educational Achievement*. A discussion paper. London: DfES.

FURTHER READING

Carr, M (2001) *Assessment in Early Childhood Settings*. London: Paul Chapman.

Clark and Moss (2001) *Listening to Young Children: The Mosaic Approach*. London: National Children's Bureau.

Easen, P, Kendall, P and Shaw, J (2007) Parents and Educators: Dialogue and Development Through Partnership. *Children & Society*, Volume 6 (4): 282–96.

Gerhardt, S (2004) *Why Love Matters*. London: Routledge.

Goldschmied, E and Jackson, S (2004) *People under Three, Young Children in Day Care* (2nd ed). London: Routledge.

Goleman, D (1996) *Emotional Intelligence*. London: Bloomsbury.

Lancaster, P and Broadbent, V (2003) *Listening to Young Children* (Coram Family). Maidenhead: Open University Press.

Manning-Morton, J and Thorp, M (2006) *Key Times: A Framework for Developing High Quality Provision for Children From Birth to Three*. Maidenhead: Open University Press.

Additional guidance

DCSF (2003, updated 2008) *Excellence and Enjoyment: Social and Emotional Aspects of Learning. Early Years Foundation Stage.* London: DCSF.

DCSF (2007) *Supporting Children Learning English as an Additional Language: Guidance for Practitioners in the Early Years Foundation Stage.* London: DCSF.

DCSF (2008) *Social and Emotional Aspects of Development: Guidance for EYFS Practitioners.* London: DCSF.

DCSF (2009) *Inclusion Development Programme-Supporting Children on the Autism Spectrum: Guidance for Practitioners in the Early Years Foundation Stage.* London: DCSF.

6 Enabling environments

Jo Basford and Lynne Clarke

CHAPTER OBJECTIVES

By the end of this chapter you should:

- *understand the observation, assessment and planning cycle and its place in learning and teaching;*
- *understand how the learning environment supports the development of young children;*
- *understand how to support the individual child in their learning journey;*
- *consider how working within the wider context supports children's individual needs.*

The chapter addresses many of the Professional Standards for QTS, but principally meets the following:
Q1; 2; 4; 5; 11; 12; 18; 19; 22; 26; 27; 28; 30; ; 32; 33.
This chapter also addresses the following Professional Standards for EYPS:
S1;6; 7; 8; 10; 21; 23.

The 'Enabling Environment' – a place to learn and develop

When you first consider the term 'environment' in any learning context, you may rightly define this as the physical aspects of the environment, such as the storage of resources and layout of furniture. The physical environment is indeed a key aspect of practice which, if planned with thought, should support children to become independent learners. The EYFS principle for Enabling Environments clearly states that *The environment plays a key role in supporting and extending children's development and learning* (EYFS, 2008). Yet this principle and the related commitments recognise that in order for the environment to genuinely enable children to reach their potential, then practitioners need to take account of aspects beyond the physical environment. An enabling environment is not just what it looks like, but also what it *feels* like.

A useful reference to this notion is captured in *The Social and Emotional Aspects of Development Guidance* (DCSF, 2008), which defines the enabling environment in the following way.

> *An enabling environment supports and promotes active learning and development for all children. It is a place where all children feel safe, cared for and relaxed because they are in the continuous care of adults who know them well and are tuned in to respond*

to their needs and interests. It involves both the physical environment – the space in which children learn and develop, and the emotional environment – the atmosphere and ethos created by all who are part of the setting.

(DCSF, 2008, page 32)

The purpose of this chapter is to explore how the four commitments concerned with enabling environments should support the overall ethos and working practices of a setting. The four commitments are:

- Observation, Assessment and Planning;

- Supporting Every Child;

- The Wider Context;

- The Learning Environment.

We will consider how these principles may be translated into practice while on your placement, and consider how you use your setting experience to support your developing knowledge, skills and understanding regarding the provision of an appropriate environment to meet children's needs.

REFLECTIVE TASK

Think back to an experience you have had when you went to a new environment for the first time. How did you feel? What made you feel comfortable? Was it the way other people greeted you and interacted with you? Was it the way the room was organised? Did someone show you around and introduce you to the systems and routines? Did all this make you feel secure?

Now consider what it is like for a young child joining a setting for the first time. When taking into account all that we know about the impact of children's well-being on their holistic development, it makes sense that this particular theme is concerned with more than just the physical layout of a setting. The manner in which adults interact with children, and the systems which are put in place to support children's time in a setting, will all have a significant impact on a child's learning and development.

3.1 Observation, assessment and planning

A key task for the Early Years practitioner is the process of observation, assessment and planning. However, how you interpret the connections between these three can be dependent on how you perceive children as learners. Anning (2007) describes conflicting discourses of the construction of children as learners. The 'folklore and tradition' of the Early Years curriculum highlights the importance of following the interests of the child. You may already have explored the influences of a range of pioneers and theorists whose work is used to justify a child-centred approach to supporting children's learning. Isaacs, Froebel and Montessori all used observation of children to gain insights into their learning and understanding. Yet, in reality, the tension created by the need to prepare children for statutory schooling and assessment can sometimes result in a tendency for adults to direct learning in order to pave the way for future success. This can lead to adults taking little account of children's own interests – particularly during child-initiated periods of play – and can result in children being given a diet of experiences that are essentially adult led. We reinforce repeatedly in this book how your placement experience may well provide you with a range of personal challenges. Within the context of this particular commitment, you may well find yourself grappling with the challenge of planning learning in a child-centred fashion while ensuring that children are prepared sufficiently for the next stage of their learning.

The EYFS explicitly refers to the importance of *starting from the child*. Practitioners are encouraged to find out about children's needs and interests as well as note how children respond to different situations. The REPEY report (a key piece of research which can be retrieved in the 'Resources' section of the EYFS CDROM) highlights the importance of the practitioner having detailed knowledge and understanding of each child, as a *professional responsibility*. The report argues that an insight into a child's social and cultural context is just as important as insight into a child's cognitive functioning. The following case study illustrates how practitioners use their observation of children's play interests as a starting point for further provision.

CASE STUDY

The nursery staff noticed that Joe and two of his friends consistently return to the construction area and play pirate games including burying treasure on an island. The adult engages with them and asks them 'how did they get it to the island'. Joe talks about a pirate ship and the adult asks what it looks like. Joe gets a book with a picture of a pirate ship and he is able to talk about a mast and sails. They decide to build a pirate ship. The adult builds on this interest and provides a range of resources including boxes, wooden sticks, string and pieces of fabric. This engages the children's interest and they work collaboratively to build their model of a pirate ship. This case study demonstrates how the adult uses ongoing observation of the children to support their future learning. She could have shared this interest with Joe's parents to find out where his interest had originated and build on this learning further.

The observation and planning cycle

The process of observation, planning and assessment is interrelated. Indeed, the Statutory Framework for the EYFS (2008, page 7) states that in order to provide a secure basis for future learning, children's learning and development is *planned around the individual needs and interests of the child and informed by the use of observational assessment*.

This means that practitioners are required to use their knowledge of the children in their setting, gained through observing them, to plan for their next steps in learning and development, which should ultimately support improved outcomes for the children in their care (see Figure 6.1 below).

Figure 6.1 The observation, assessment and planning cycle

Source: EYFS CDROM

Therefore, there are three steps in this process:

1 *Observing* the children in a variety of contexts and situations.

2 Analysing the observation (making an *assessment*). This involves thinking about what new information the observation is possibly telling you about a child's interests, involvement, motivation and capability.

3 Using this information and knowledge to help you *plan* for future experiences. This not only includes specific activities, but also resources and routines.

You will notice that practitioners in your placement setting regularly observe children. From these observations staff will be making judgements of children's learning, including their ideas, knowledge, motivation, interests, abilities and thinking. Being armed with this knowledge of the children will help them to ensure that the resources and activities, both indoors and outdoors, are inspiring, challenging and intriguing. Involve yourself in this process, and in the first instance adopt the setting's own systems for observing children. You need to be willing to share the information you have gained with the rest of the staff and this will include any information from child studies you may have to complete as part of your assessment.

Ethical issues

One of the first things you will need to consider is how you gain access and permission to observe a child from parents/carers and then how you will support their understanding of the purpose and outcomes of the observations. While it is difficult to seek informed permission from babies and toddlers, you may wish to consider ways in which you can seek permission with older children. The issue of confidentiality and anonymity should also be considered and you may choose to use only the first name or initials to ensure this. You also need to think about how and where the observations are stored.

The key person observes Emma at the painting easel. She paints a group of four figures – two adults and two children. She paints features such as eyes, mouth and nose on each figure. She gives each figure, fingers and 'shoes', a head but no body. She selects yellow paint and gives one figure blond hair. She spends an extended amount of time at this activity, which is self-chosen.

The key person notes that Emma has shown an interest in drawing similar figures using different drawing tools at the mark-making table, but she notes that Emma's drawing is becoming more detailed and her fine manipulative strokes are more refined.

The key person completes spontaneous observation and adds it to the child's profile. She talks to the rest of the team members about the possibility of enhancing the provision of mark-making resources by offering a wider range of paper and tools for all the children, and providing a mark-making box that can be taken outside by the children.

During your placement, choose a child and carry out regular observations. Use the pointers below to help you to determine what is significant about what you have observed.

- The child has demonstrated a skill for the first time.
- You believe the child has mastered a concept after demonstrating proficiency on several occasions and across a range of contexts.
- The achievement may be significant for a particular child e.g. a child with speech or language difficulties may initiate a conversation for the first time.
- Talking to the child about their achievements so they are able to consider its significance.

If it is truly a significant achievement then you will need to consider the implications for the future planning of learning opportunities for that child.

The nature and purpose of observation

The more knowledge the adult has of the child the better matched their support and the more effective the subsequent learning.

(REPEY, Siraj-Blatchford et al., 2002)

Through observations you should be able to:

- find out more about the child/children you are working with – their likes, dislikes, their reactions to change or new situations, as well as the stage they are at in their learning and development;
- recognise each child as an individual and find out about specific needs;
- ensure your subsequent planning is based on the needs of the child/children;
- put the child at the centre of your practice.

Observations should include children:

● engaged in child-initiated activities;

● engaged in adult-initiated activities and adult-led activities;

● learning indoors and outdoors.

The Leuven Involvement and Wellbeing Scale (Laevers,1996) is a useful observation method to determine children's level of involvement. This method looks at a list of involvement signals and levels of involvement on a 5-point scale, and places particular emphasis on children's level of well-being and engagement with their play. It is a particularly useful tool if you are interested in how children play. For example, levels of concentration and perseverance may well be different when a child is engaged in self-initiated rather than adult-initiated play.

Observation is time-consuming, and there needs to be a careful balance between time spent involved directly with children supporting their learning, and time spent indirectly observing learning. These roles are complementary, but there are times when we can become 'observation obsessed' without really thinking about the reasons behind why we are making copious notes of children's actions. The key to the process is not *the quantity of observations but on the quality and significance gained* (Hutchin, 2007, page 45). You will need to develop your skill in capturing significant moments that are worthy of recording, as well as the pre-planned opportunities. Chapter 5 discusses the significance of the key person, and the value of the close relationship built with key children, and it is this relationship that will enable you to know when something a particular child does is significant and unique to their own learning and development.

What formats might you use to record the observations?
Settings will use a range of observation strategies, and the type of observation you undertake is usually determined by the nature of information you wish to illicit. Although it is important that you adopt the approach the setting uses, you may well also need to use some different strategies in order to successfully complete any tasks you have been set by your college/university.

The following types of observations can be used to record what you have seen.

Participant observation	A record of what you see the child do or say when you are involved in play with children.
Incidental or anecdotal observation	A record (sometimes a very brief narrative) of something significant during everyday activities that is significant to that child.
Audio/video or photographic evidence	A useful tool to observe verbal and non-verbal communication, or to capture a more holistic event. Practitioners have annotated the significant learning or conversations with children.

▶

Samples of children's work	To include, drawings, samples of emergent writing, photographs of models, which over a period of time identify progress.
Planned or focused observations	To include narrative, coded, tracking or sampling. These may be carried out to look at particular aspects of practice or to observe and seek information concerning a potential concern for child's progress.

Table 6.1 A range of observation strategies

There is some skill required to write a valid observation, and with practice you will become more proficient at writing objective and factual observations, which are useful. For the observations to be meaningful and used effectively it is important to include the following information:

- The date.

- The time the observation took place.

- The duration of the observation.

- The context.

Look at the following observation, and note how the practitioner only records what she actually saw and heard. The effectiveness of the observation is self-evident in the evaluation, which enables the team to identify the child's capability and interests, and also consider how this information helps to support planning for the child's future learning. Imagine the further potential in supporting her learning if this observation was shared with the child's parents.

Observation
Child A   Age: 2 years 3 months   Date: 6.1.10   Duration: 10 mins
Context: Puzzle table (self-chosen)
Child A selects animal jigsaw from shelf. Using her right hand, she picks up the inset pieces and matches them to the correct picture. She talks to herself as she matches the pieces, naming the animals as she does. She finishes one puzzle and starts a second one. She remains engaged with the puzzles for 10 minutes.

What does this show about A's learning?
She uses her right hand consistently. She is able to work independently, and is able to concentrate in a self-chosen activity. She is able to recognise and correctly name farm animals – sheep, cow, pig, horse and chicken.

Implications for future planning
Provide other matching activities. Move on to 4–6 piece puzzles. Ensure farm animals and books are available to play with.

The CDROM of the EYFS includes a broad range of formats for a further method of recording, this includes *Learning Stories*, which are referred to in greater depth in the next section.

The connection between observation and planning

The earlier planning cycle identifies the link between observations and planning and the EYFS CDROM, Enabling Environment 3.1 Observation, Assessment and Planning, provides several exemplars of planning for individual needs. However, as many settings continue to use a topic-based approach, one of the challenges you may encounter is planning to meet individual needs. It is not practical to provide plans for each child. However, Percival (2010) usefully suggests a more pragmatic approach, which encourages practitioners to use their observation and assessment information to build up a picture of children's interests, learning styles, skills and knowledge. This in turn can then inform your interactions with children, the resourcing of the environment and the ways you group children, to support their learning.

3.2 Supporting every child

> Children are born with a genetic blueprint that maps their growth, but their learning and development are not fixed. The environments in which children grow up in have a strong influence on what they do and what they can accomplish. These environments are made up of a multitude of different influences such as places, cultures and people that each child comes into contact with from day to day, month to month and year to year.
>
> (DCSF, 2007, *Effective Practice: Supporting Every Child*, page 1)

This statement exemplifies the complexity of each child's pattern of experiences, which can shape and define their own individual learning journey. A useful connection can be made here with Brofenbrenner's (1979) ecological model of development. Barron (2005) explains how the interactions between a child and 'significant others' at the micro level of the family; the impact of communities and institutions (such as an Early Years setting) at the meso and exo level; and the cultural, political, religious, moral and economic imperatives that govern life at the level of any given society all have some significance to a child's development. This commitment encourages you to consider how best you can support children's own pathways of learning and development, taking into account the range of relationships and interactions a child encounters.

The term 'learning journey' is now synonymous with Early Years practice. In a broad sense, the term is used generally to describe a child's encounters with familiar and new experiences, and their responses. This term is, however, more commonly used in settings to define the process of documenting children's learning, usually exemplified by photographs and annotation of a particular aspect of a child's learning (sometimes referred to as a 'learning story').

Settings are increasingly making use of the learning journey/story to record individual children's interests and progress and to identify future experiences and activities to support their learning. While on your placement you may well see this form of documentation used in a variety of ways.

The learning story is a narrative observation which:

- describes: *what learning is taking place*

- documents: *some of the actions*

- promotes: discussion between practitioners, parents and the learner

- focuses: next steps.

There are two key international influences on documentation in the UK. The learning story was originally developed by Margaret Carr (2001) and based on the New Zealand Curriculum *Te Whariki*. This has been referred to by Luff (2007) as the long-standing tradition of parents and practitioners readily exchanging their own observations of children's learning, which has now been formalised as a 'learning story' approach to documenting learning.

The notion of documentation through a wide range of texts such as photographs, drawing and transcripts is the well-known system within the Reggio Emilia approach in Italy. Rather than it being used as a traditional tool for analysing children's development, it is used as Luff (2007, page 187) describes as a *dynamic collaborative enterprise in which the child is an active participant and parents and others may become engaged*. There is a subtle difference to the two approaches. It could be argued that both are concerned with co-construction of meaning, but through different voices. The New Zealand approach places an emphasis on the information shared between the setting and home providing a full understanding of a child's learning. Alternatively, the Reggio Emilia approach is firmly grounded in the relationship between the adult and child and the sense the child is deriving from a learning experience.

The quotation at the beginning of this section reminds you of the way this particular commitment emphasises the importance of the environment that we create for a child's learning journey, and of the need to be mindful that it is made up of multiple influences, including the child's environment *beyond* the setting. Good practice involves a close involvement with a child's parents/carers to share a child's learning journey. This may include formal/informal times to talk about a child's learning journey, and an authentic involvement of the family in the process. Photographs, materials and other information from home can help to provide a more accurate picture of each child's unique learning journey.

CHALLENGES and DILEMMAS

The fundamental difference in documenting children's learning in the UK, compared to other international approaches, is the need to provide evidence of children's learning against a standardised set of outcomes (namely the Early Learning Goals). There is no prescribed curriculum in either New Zealand or Italy, which in turn means there is no prescribed amount or type of documentation required.

continued

The setting in which you have been placed is challenged with the task of providing meaningful evidence of children's learning, which genuinely takes account of the contribution of a child's whole environment. Alongside this, practitioners are required to reflect upon the child's learning, and consider the possible next steps.

If your placement uses learning journeys, how are they used to supporting learning and planning for further experiences?

● *To what extent is the process of documenting learning useful and beneficial (to the child, parent and practitioner)?*

● *Can you identify any barriers to the success of this process, followed by possible solutions?*

3.3 The learning environment

This particular commitment is concerned with the ***emotional***, ***outdoor*** and ***indoor*** environments.

The physical layout and design of an Early Years setting can sometimes be misleading in terms of the actual quality of experience provided for children. It is true that first impressions count, but a glossy, colour co-ordinated environment with shiny new equipment and purpose-built play things is not necessarily going to provide any more appropriate experience for children than a local pre-school which is run in the community centre, where equipment is set out every day, and is of varying degrees of age and type. It is the adults in a setting who create the emotional environment, and when children feel they are accepted and supported, they will then be confident to utilise the learning environment provided for them. Many connections can be made in this section with Chapter 5, with particular consideration of the importance of attachment and the key person.

An enabling environment is about creating a positive environment, typically defined as an 'ethos' or culture. It is not always easy to define the 'ethos' of a setting, but Blandford and Knowles (2009) define this as a community which has its own characteristics and personality. They describe a number of ways in which the culture of a setting can be described:

● *Practice: rites, ritual and ceremonies* – such as how children are welcomed on a daily basis.

● *Communications: stories, legends, symbols and slogans* – such as pictures and slogans on displays, which are accessible and relevant to the children and families who use the settings.

● *Physical forms*: location, style and condition of the building, fixtures and fittings – is the building a clean and inviting place to be?

● *Common language*: phrases or jargon common to the setting – are certain words employed to describe areas in the setting, e.g. 'messy area' for art table?

(Adapted from Blandford and Knowles, 2009, page 25)

You may find this a useful starting point to help you gain a sense of the unique culture of your own placement setting. By examining this, it should help to give you an insight into the values and behaviours of the practitioners who work in the setting. These, in turn, will be reflected in the policies and practices you observe.

PRACTICAL TASK

Look at the four key points that are outlined in 'the emotional environment' section of Principle into Practice card 3.3. These help to illustrate the type of values and behaviours that can support a child in dealing with emotions associated with conflict, risk and change.

Now think particularly about your placement setting. Can you exemplify what the setting does in relation to the four key points, which help to create an appropriate emotional environment?

The EYFS card 3.3 (DCFS, 2008) states: *A rich and varied environment supports children's learning and development. It gives them the confidence to explore and learn in secure and safe, yet challenging, indoor and outdoor spaces.*

At this point, you can make some useful connections with the theme and commitments related to **Learning and Development** in Chapter 5. This particular theme is based on the notion of child-centred learning, influenced by constructivist (Piaget) and social constructivist (Vygotsky and Bruner) theory. Westernised pedagogical practices readily accept that children learn through active, first-hand experiences. It therefore makes sense that the physical environment we create for children needs to allow for opportunities for children to use a wide range of materials in a wide range of ways in accordance with their own interest and learning needs. The design of the physical environment therefore needs to make sense to a child.

The High/scope approach places significant emphasis on the learning environment, stating that *young children need spaces that are arranged and equipped to promote active learning* (Hohmann and Weikart,1995, page 111). Yet this idea goes beyond the traditional notion of the physical layout of the environment, and storage of materials. Practitioners are also encouraged to consider the type of materials available for children to use, which reflect their interests, and are suitably 'open ended' so that they can be used in a variety of ways. Hohmann and Weikart (1995) provide detailed and very thoughtful guidance around 'Arranging and equipping spaces for active learners', which you may find useful when considering this particular aspect of practice on your placement (see Further Reading at the end of this chapter). You may also wish to look at the information provided by Community Playthings on planning the environment.

CHALLENGES and DILEMMAS

Some settings may operate from a shared building where furniture, equipment and resources have to be set out and put away each time, but staff will still need to create a comfortable and welcoming environment. They will still need to consider how to provide distinct areas within the room; provide space and opportunities to display children's work; store materials and resources in such a way that children freely have access; and provide quite comfortable areas for children to rest or be quiet.

The outdoor environment

It is common to hear in the field of Early Years that everything that happens indoors can be replicated outdoors. The fact that children are exposed to fresh air, larger, less confined spaces, and equipment which enables them to physically exert themselves means that it is a different experience to learning indoors. Children may feel less restricted, and therefore more comfortable to take risks and express themselves in other ways that are deemed less acceptable within the confines of an indoor space.

Nevertheless, outdoor provision should not be just concerned with physical play. The 'ideal' notion of an effective learning environment is described in the EYFS as *the space both indoors and outdoors should preferably be available all the time so children can choose activities and follow their interests* (2008, *Effective Practice: The Learning Environment*, page 1). Many Early Years settings are faced with a variety of barriers which make it difficult to provide for seamless opportunities to move between indoor and outdoor play. Staffing ratios and access are two common challenges to be met.

When considering the design, layout and materials available in the outdoor environment, the same High/scope principles can be applied. It is important that a range of play opportunities is accommodated outside. Sometimes, settings have to be very creative and it can mean a lot of physical movement of resources, equipment and people to enable children to utilise the space available as effectively as possible. Many settings find creative ways of providing opportunities for outdoor provision. For example, some settings are fortunate enough to be involved in the Forest Schools Movement, which provides opportunities for children to spend time in specially created spaces in forests, woodland areas or natural spaces located within the premises of the setting. You may wish to research this approach further. Also, the work of Bilton (2002) provides a great deal of rich guidance and theory to support practice in the outdoor environment.

The learning environment and under-threes

In some settings you may be working with children under three and you will need to consider how to meet the needs of these young children. Babies and toddlers will benefit from an environment where they are able to *look, listen, wiggle, roll, crawl, climb, rock, bounce, rest, eat, make noise, grasp or mouth or drop things, and be messy from time to time* (Post and Hohmann, 2000).

While there is a wide variety of commercially produced toys, you will want to consider how they can be used flexibly to support children's learning and enjoyment and whether other natural or everyday objects may support children's learning and achievement equally well. Eleanor Goldschmied (1987) pioneered treasure baskets, as a form of heuristic play – a term used to describe exploratory play with boxes, jars and various containers. Treasure basket-type activities are a traditional pedagogical approach for working with under-threes and you may have opportunities to reflect on how this resource can be used to support learning.

Babies and toddlers will need a comfortable space to rest or sleep. Some settings take a formal approach to sleep patterns and routines, where most children tend to fit in with the routine of the setting. Alternatively, some settings may take a more flexible approach, which allows children to sleep where and when they are most comfortable. In either system, each child will need individual bedding and very often their own 'comfort object' to help them settle.

Continuous and enhanced provision

Nutbrown (2006) talks about the importance of consistency in the experiences and materials in children's learning environment. This provides a sense of familiarity and comfort to children, and means that they can revisit their learning to reinforce earlier ideas and concepts or to build on and adapt their thinking. This consistency of experiences and materials that are the basic offering in the setting every day can be described as 'continuous provision'. The range of continuous provision areas which are commonly found in Early Years settings may include sensory play, messy play, role play, mark-making, physical play, construction, story or book area.

When you take time to interpret the observations of children's learning in your setting, you may well see some recurring patterns and themes in children's interests, schematic behaviours or types of play. You might respond to this by adding to or 'enhancing' the provision by adding new materials, adapting play spaces or amending the daily routine for a period of time.

An example of a pro-forma to support the development of continuous provision can be found in Nutbrown and Page (2008) Chapter 4, page 80.

Alternative formats can also be found on the EYFS CDROM in the resources section in Enabling Environments 3.1 Observation, Assessment and Planning.

3.4 The wider context

The final commitment within this theme is very closely connected to the theme Positive Relationships, as it is concerned with how partnerships with other settings, professionals and individuals or groups in the community support children's development and progress towards the outcomes of ECM (EYFS, Principle into Practice card 3.4).

When taking into account the wider context in which a child exists, it is useful to refer back to Brofenbrenners's (1979) portrayal of the child at the centre of an interconnected set of contexts or microsystems (Fabian and Dunlop, 2002). Within the varied context in which a child exists, they will experience a range of **transitions** from either day to day, or over time. Neuman (2002) describes these as either *vertical* (such as from nursery to school) or *horizontal*, from one setting to another within a day. One of the key challenges practitioners face is finding ways to ensure there is a sense of **continuity** for all children during any transition process.

Movement from the unique culture of one setting to another can be an unsettling experience for any child. Many children are exposed to at least two different contexts daily, home to nursery/school. Other children may also experience care in an out-of- hours context, either with extended family, home-based care or after-school provision. Children will be expected to adapt to different people, routines, boundaries and expectations. Chapter 5 provides you with an opportunity to reflect on the theory related to attachment and shared care, which are significant to this particular commitment.

Although the EYFS highlights that children and parents can be reassured when *they find that each setting incorporates the same values and that learning continues within a familiar context* (2008, Effective Practice: The Wider Context, page 2), this is not always going to be the case. Taking a reflective approach towards transitional issues will mean that you will have a greater awareness of the impact of transition and how best you can support children through the transition process.

PRACTICAL TASK

Research the settling-in and transition policy within the setting.

- *What information from parents is used to support child's transition?*
- *How is the child and family introduced into to the setting?*
- *What information is provided for parents about the practice and ethos of the setting? Who provides this information?*
- *If the setting has a key person system how is he/she involved in supporting the settling-in process?*
- *How does the setting work with other professionals and contexts to ensure continuity of experience for the child?*

Working in partnership with other professionals is seen as a key aspect of working towards the five outcomes of ECM. **Multi-agency working** involves looking at children's needs holistically, and ensuring that all the services involved with a child's learning and development share information and provide appropriate support as soon as a need is identified. It is important that settings find ways of communicating with each other to ensure the experience for a child is as seamless as possible. This is not always going to be easy. For example, there are sometimes time and distance restraints, which make contact difficult. There will also be occasions when support for individual children becomes more specialised, and identified professionals work with the child and family. Effective information-sharing processes are essential, as well as an appropriate mindset that demonstrates professionalism and respect for all parties (see Chapter 5 for further insight).

Some placements will provide you with an opportunity to see effective multi-agency working in practice. Children's Centres, and schools fully engaged in the extended schools agenda, should provide you with some interesting first-hand experiences. Many nurseries and pre-schools particularly have much less access to other professionals unless one of the children is receiving targeted support for a specific condition or need. It is, therefore, your responsibility to take a proactive approach in researching how your setting works with other agencies.

Your placement setting is situated within its own unique **community** and will have links with other groups, and services, such as the library and health centre and other religious and cultural groups. Working closely with the local community not only helps you to make authentic links with children's own worlds beyond the setting, but also helps to provide a network of support and communication between all stakeholders.

C H A P T E R   S U M M A R Y

Children exist in a range of interconnected contexts. The experiences they are exposed to are not always consistent. It is the role of the Early Years practitioner to provide an enabling environment that takes account of a child's life beyond the setting. This involves developing effective systems for observation, assessment and planning which allows for Early Years practitioners to work closely with all stakeholders to follow each child's unique learning journey. The physical and emotional environment should be created in such a way that children are supported to feel valued and safe, as well as inspired and motivated to explore, take risks and make sense of the world in which they live.

REFERENCES

Anning, A (2007) Play and the Legislated Curriculum: Back to Basics: an alternative view, in Moyles, J (ed.) *The Excellence of Play* (2nd ed.) Maidenhead: Open University Press.

Barron, I (2005) Understanding Development in Early Childhood, in Jones, L, Holmes, R and Powell, J *A Multi-professional Perspective*. Maidenhead: Open University Press.

Bilton, H (2002) *Outdoor Play in the Early Years* (2nd ed). London: David Fulton Publishing.

Blandford, S and Knowles, C (2009) *Developing Professional Practice 0–7*. Harlow: Pearson Education Limited.

Brofenbrenner, U (1979) *The Ecology of Human Development: Experiments by Nature and Design*. Cambridge, MA: Harvard University Press.

Carr, M (2001) *Assessment in Early Years Settings*. London: Paul Chapman Publishing.

DCSF (2007) *Effective Practice: Supporting Every Child*. London: DCSF.

DCSF (2008) *Social and Emotional Aspects of Development: Guidance for EYFS Practitioners*. London: DCSF.

Fabian, H and Dunlop, W (eds) (2002) *Transitions in The Early Years*. London: Routledge Falmer.

Goldschmied, E (1987) *Infants at work* (training video). London: National Children's Bureau.

Hohmann, M and Weikart, D (1995) *Educating Young Children*. Michigan: High Scope Press.

Hutchin, V (2007) *Supporting Every Child's Learning across the Early Years Foundation Stage*. London: Hodder Education.

Laevers, F (1996) *The Leuven Involvement Scale for Young Children LIS-YC*. Manual and Video Tape, Experiential Education Series No 1. Leuven, Belgium: Centre for Experiential Education.

Luff, P (2007) Documenting Children's Experiences, in Moyles, J (ed) *Early Years Foundations. Meeting the Challenge*. Maidenhead: Open University Press.

Neuman, M (2002) The Wider Context. An International Overview of Transition Issues, in Fabian, H and Dunlop, W (eds) *Transitions in The Early Years*. London: Routledge Falmer.

Nutbrown, C (2006) *Threads of Thinking* (3rd ed). London: Sage.

Nutbrown, C and Page, J (2008) *Working with Babies and Children*. London: Sage.

Percival, J (2010) Personalised Learning: Looking at Children Holistically, in Glazzard, J, Chadwick, D, Webster, A and Percival, J *Assessment in the Early Years Foundation Stage*. London: Sage.

Post, J and Hohmann, M (2000) *Tender Care and Early Learning*. Ypsilanti, MI: High Scope.

Sylva, K, Melhuish, E, Sammons, P, Siraj-Blatchford, I, Taggart, B and Elliot, K (2003) *The Effective Provision of Pre-school Education (EPPE) Project*. London: Institute of Education.

FURTHER READING

Bilton, H (2004) *Playing Outside Activities, Ideas and Inspiration for the Early Years*. London: David Fulton Publishing.

Hohmann, M and Weikart, D (1995) *Educating Young Children*. Michigan: High Scope Press. Part 2, chapter 5.

7 Learning and development

Elaine Hodson

CHAPTER OBJECTIVES

By the end of this chapter you will have learnt:

- *how you can support young children's learning and development during your placement;*
- *the key pedagogical features of the educator's role in supporting learning.*

This chapter addresses the following Professional Standards for QTS and EYPS:
QTS: Q1; 3a; 14; 15; 18; 19.
EYPS: S1; 2; 3; 7; 11; 14; 16; 31; 39.

Introduction

Learning and Development is one of the four themes underpinning the EYFS Practice Guidance. As a practitioner on placement in an Early Years setting you will need to begin to make links between the theory you have already begun acquiring about the way young children learn and develop, and the practice you are experiencing in the setting in which you have been placed. Although the diversity between settings will impact on the experience you have, whatever type of setting you find yourself placed in, the young learners you are working with are entitled to high quality opportunities that will enhance their learning and development. Chapter 1 outlines the wide range of settings covered by the EYFS, and the historical factors that have influenced provision for under-fives in England. A key purpose of the Practice Guidance, (and of the earlier Curriculum Guidance for the Foundation Stage (QCA/DfEE, 2000) which pre-dated it), lies in, *setting Standards for Learning, Development and Care for all children from birth to five,* regardless of the Early Years setting in which they are placed. The practitioners who work in each of these settings are expected to work together within this framework to provide high quality, play-based learning opportunities. The result of this is to overcome the inequalities historically present in different types of settings and to improve transition for children who may receive care in more than one setting, as well as improving transition at the end of a child's period in a setting.

The four principles underlying this theme are that children learn:

- in different ways;

- at different rates;

- that children need to be encouraged to see connections in their learning;

- that all areas of learning are equally important and interconnected.

It is these principles that we will explore in this chapter while at the same time beginning to consider the implications for you as a practitioner as you start to take responsibility for the Learning and Development of the children in your care.

Learning in different ways and at different rates

The EYFS places the child at the centre of the learning process. It describes learners competent from birth, able to learn by following their interests and by interacting with others. Babies are characterised by their motivation to explore and to make contact. The form this exploration takes changes as children grow and develop. It is part of your role as a practitioner to tune into the learners around you and to become increasingly aware of the huge differences in the way they learn and develop. This chapter is designed to help you develop that awareness.

The importance of play and exploration

A strength of the EYFS Practice Guidance is that it draws its foundations from an extensive body of research and theory. You will find links to this material on the EYFS resources section [online].

This chapter does not use the EYFS themes and commitments as section headings, because in this chapter the commitments are much more interconnected and become difficult to separate discretely. Instead, the following section is intended as a brief introduction to some of these ideas.

If you are to become an effective practitioner, you will need to be able to use your developing knowledge, skills and understanding to make sense of the practice around you (this is discussed in more detail in Chapter 2). To the untrained eye, children in EYFS settings may appear to be achieving little. Indeed, practitioners have long had to defend their practice against charges that EYFS settings are 'chaotic'. They are also often told that their job is easy, because young children 'just play', implying that practitioners working with young children are simply bystanders with no pedagogic responsibilities. If you are to begin to see beyond these simplified criticisms, and indeed to begin to articulate your own role in this important work, you will need to familiarise yourself with the research and theory associated with children learning through play.

Interest in the importance of play for the development of thinking and learning was first documented in the eighteenth and nineteenth centuries. Writers such as Froebel, Montessori and Isaacs used their own work with young children to inform their thinking. Many of their ideas about play, learning by doing, and the importance of sensitive adult intervention, continue to be held as true today as when they were first written and have done much to influence the principles and commitments of the EYFS Practice Guidance. However, some would argue that these historical viewpoints do little to justify play as a tool for learning. During the twentieth century, psychoanalytical theories from Freud and Erikson added some contribution by identifying that the way children play may support them in coming to terms with their worlds. However, it was work by the Swiss scientist

Piaget (1955) that first fuelled the concept that play was significant in children's learning. As a scientist, Piaget was interested in the way in which all organisms live, develop, and evolve through their relationship with their environments. He extended his study to include human development by studying his own children. Piaget developed a theory that children, in common with other developing creatures, needed opportunities to interact with the world around them. His work made clear that young children could not learn simply by being told, they needed to mobilise all their senses in order to make sense of their environment. He suggested that children acquired knowledge by activating all their senses. He then argued that they developed new concepts, or schemas, by assimilating knowledge, skills or understanding into their existing ideas about the world. In order to store this new information, the learner then needed to find a way to accommodate it alongside existing knowledge. Where new concepts or schema appeared not to fit with existing knowledge the learner would be in a stage of disequilibration, literally, out of balance. The learner, he believed, remained in this stage of disequilibration until new ideas could be made to fit with old concepts. Piaget argued that it was at this point of disequilibration that new learning took place. Piaget also argued that children's understanding passed through series of qualitatively different stages and that these stages were age related. He labelled these, sensori-motor, from birth to two years, pre-operational from two to seven years, concrete operations from seven to eleven and formal operations from eleven onwards. During each of these stages, Piaget believed children required different learning environments, the sensori-motor learner needed activities to stimulate the senses, while the learners in the concrete operational stage needed problem-solving activities which employed concrete objects. Piaget's ideas had a strong impact on teaching in mid-twentieth century England, with its strongest influence being felt in the Plowden Report (Central Advisory Council for Education (England), 1967). Critics have since argued that Piagetian thinking disempowered teachers since it ushered in the notion that they should provide a stimulating environment and then stand back in order for the child to explore and, thereby, learn. Indeed, Piagetians maintained that any attempt to move children's learning forward more quickly than their development determined could have a positively detrimental effect.

Donaldson (1978), however, reworked some of the experiments that Piaget had used to establish his theories, for example, the process of matching objects to establish one-to-one correspondence. She argued that when she provided children with meaningful contexts for the problems she was presenting to them, they responded in line with Piaget's more sophisticated stages of thinking. So, when she suggested that the objects had all been mixed up by a 'naughty teddy' the children showed much more engagement with the sorting task. She referred to the need for children to see 'human sense' in the problems being posed.

Work on the way schema may inform children's thinking was carried out later by Athey (1990), who was particularly interested in the practical application of this process and the way parents might support learner's development. While this section has provided only brief account of Piaget's work, you will already see how the EYFS principles draw on his work. If children are active learners, then it follows that they must be given some control of the way they learn and the rate at which they move in their learning.

Child-initiated learning

The idea that children should at times be able to organise their own learning is, therefore, central to the EYFS Practice Guidance. One reason that EYFS contexts may appear chaotic to the untrained eye, in the way described earlier, is the way young learners are empowered to make choices. Observing in an EYFS setting, you will quickly become aware of the huge variety of learning experiences that children may be engaged in. This may stand in stark contrast to some of the more formal learning contexts you may have previously seen provided for children of the same age, or slightly older, or may even have experienced yourself as a young learner. The following table may help you consider the possible contrasting features.

Formal learning environment	Informal learning environment
Children arranged in a large group with limited opportunities for interaction with an adult	Children working individually, in pairs, or in small groups, sometimes working with adults, sometimes working independently
Learning environment composed mainly of tables and chairs	Learning taking place both indoors and out and, where possible with children moving freely between the two
Children generally still and emphasis is placed on sitting, listening, reading and writing	Children are sitting, listening, reading and writing, but are also standing, lying on the floor, climbing, dancing, running or walking
Timetabling carves learning times into regulated slots and discrete subjects	Learners are presented with extended periods of time to move between areas where different and varied learning opportunities are being made available. Adults encourage learners to return to and revisit activities in order to extend and refine work

Table 7.1 A comparison of formal and informal learning environments

Occasionally, you may observe practitioners gathering large groups of children together for specific experiences. In some Reception classes you may find this becomes more common in the Summer Term when features of the Key Stage 1 Primary Curriculum may begin to influence practice.

> **REFLECTIVE TASK**
>
> *As a practitioner working in the EYFS, you will be expected to ensure that the children in your care make good progress in their development and learning. How do your colleagues ensure that this happens? What knowledge and skills will you need to develop in order to become adept at this?*

As your eye becomes trained, and your observational abilities develop, you will be able not only to identify how and what these children are learning, but also become adept at identifying the next steps for them. What you will begin to appreciate is that young learners do indeed learn in different ways and at different rates and that it is your responsibility to provide for this.

So that practitioners ensure that they engage the maximum number of learners when they present an activity, they, and you, need to ensure that you make learning accessible to learners who employ different ways of learning. Evidence suggests that all individuals, but young learners in particular, learn through a range of sensory channels: visual, auditory and kinaesthetic. Traditional teaching has often relied on the auditory channel, with adults telling children and expecting them to listen and to learn. It is becoming increasingly clear that some learning takes place through looking, while other learning relies on handling or physical experience. Some learners seem to learn more through one particular channel, and some learning experiences lend themselves more effectively to different learning requirements. So, if you are to ensure children have opportunities to be actively involved, you will need to plan learning that incorporates a range of approaches.

PRACTICAL TASK

With your mentor, select a child to track for half a day. Make a note of the different learning activities she becomes involved in. Which sensory channels is she employing? Do the same ones repeat, or do they vary? Does she seem to learn using all channels or are some more effective than others?

Working with parents and carers

In order to ensure that you plan appropriately to meet the individual learning needs of learners, you will need to get to know the children in your care well. You will become aware of the children who love noise and excitement, and those who prefer a quieter, more measured approach. If you are to personalise learning you will need to tune into children's interests in order to engage and motivate them. Chapter 6 takes you through the significance of formative assessment in tracking progress and planning next steps in learning. In order to underpin this process, you will need to draw on the knowledge of those who already know these children well, their parents and carers. Chapter 5 explains the significance of building these productive relationships in order to support learning.

The role of the adult

The more your trained eye observes your colleagues in your placement, the more you will also begin to appreciate the highly skilled role of these adults as they manage and develop learning across all six areas within the EYFS context. You will see practitioners maintaining a balance between child-initiated and adult-initiated learning. You will also become aware of the highly skilled way in which they build on and extend this learning. It is this significant role that has been the focus of educationalists who began to challenge the Piagetian viewpoint. In the 1970s, the work of the Russian psychologist, Vygotsky, was translated into English. Vygotsky (1978) held that learning took place through social interaction with others. Vygotsky suggested that new learning takes place in the Zone of Proximal Development (ZPD). He argued that when a learner was supported by another individual, who had already acquired some knowledge skill or understanding, the learner could move forward in their thinking and operate within the ZPD. Vygotsky argues that this support might be lent by an adult, or by a more advanced peer. Interestingly, he saw play experiences as providing most effective opportunities for learners to take risks and to operate in the ZPD. This process of support has seen been referred to later by Bruner (1978) as scaffolding. The important thing for you is that Vygotsky depicts a highly significant role for the educator. While Piaget saw learners as controlling their own individual learning, which 'teachers' could only facilitate, Vygotsky believed that learners had the capacity to learn through instruction.

Adults as scaffolders

The concept of adults scaffolding learning is one that you will probably hear discussed in your setting. The difficulty for you may be that it is a term so widely used that it may not be clearly defined, and different individuals may hold different interpretations. When Bruner defined this term he was trying to label the process whereby effective educators develop their skills of breaking down new learning into a process of small achievable steps, which the learner is gradually able to master. This may make most sense to you if you think about a child trying to master a task such as completing a jigsaw. The scaffolder would make a series of suggestions such as:

● let's turn over the pieces so we can see the picture-side;

● let's stand the box up so we can see the picture;

● can we find the corner pieces?

● can we find all the straight pieces to go around the edge?

● here's a piece with lots of red on it, could it be part of her coat?

Each suggestion would be accompanied by a physical intervention modified to take account of the child's reaction. If the child struggles, for example, to find a corner, the adult might initially pick it up. On a second occasion, the adult might point to a relevant piece, while on a third occasion they may 'eye-point' or offer other clues to its position. Throughout, sensitive scaffolding of the process would depend on the adult continually monitoring the learner's reaction – providing more support as the child struggles, less support as the child begins to employ their own initiative. This is a process that involves the gradual transferral of control over the task from the supported to the learner.

Scaffolding a learner successfully requires the educator to be highly attentive and tuned in to the learner's responses. Wood (1986) discusses the features of successful scaffolding. Coining the term 'contingent' to identify the most effective support provided by the most successful educators, he studied the process and argued that they demonstrated in their interactions the most important features of scaffolding. He argued that if the learner began to fail at the task, the adult immediately offered more support, to prevent failure taking place. Conversely, as the child became more successful, the adult reduced their support and handed greater control of the task to the learner. Wood identified teaching contingently to be highly challenging, and found that even when educators were trained in making contingent responses (for teaching one specific task), they succeeded in making responding contingently on only 85 per cent of opportunities. Wood's work was focused on scaffolding a specific task on a one-to-one basis. He concluded that since teaching contingently was a highly challenging task, the possibility of teachers in classroom situations working with large numbers of learners being able to make contingent responses, was minimal. Unsurprisingly he discovered that parents and carers were more adept than teachers at responding contingently.

The learning environment

By now you will be beginning to recognise the responsibility for both planning and resourcing the learning environment that the practitioners in a setting share. You will find more in-depth discussion of this in Chapter 6. In this section we will consider the practitioners' professional responsibility for ensuring that all children in their care receive high quality learning opportunities. In order for this to be the case, several conditions must be satisfied.

- The children will need to be motivated to learn.

- Learning opportunities must be accessible.

- Opportunities will need to be available to make links to prior learning.

- Careful assessment will be needed to ensure that new learning is matched to development.

- Continual evaluation will be needed to ensure that learning and teaching are effectively managed.

At this point, it suffices to say that the environment must be stimulating if children are to experience the desire to become involved in learning and to interact with others. A challenge for the practitioner lies in managing that environment in order to maintain a balance between working on focused activities with individuals and groups, and maintaining an overview of the whole provision. On a macro level, the educator must ensure that resources remain attractive and accessible, that children remain safe and secure but challenged, and that there is sufficient range to ensure that all children are able to access learning. In order for you to learn to monitor in this way, you will need to develop what Moyles (1989) describes as the *visual sweep*, an ability to monitor and record both the environment around you and the learning taking place. Planning effectively will require you to hold in your head a wealth of information about each child concerning their interests, abilities, and levels of development. Since most EYFS contexts will be staffed by a number of adults, strategies to ensure there are good channels of communication are vital, since effective teamwork is essential to planning, evaluating and assessing learning. Depending on your role in the setting, it may be your responsibility to begin to manage others to ensure these outcomes are achieved. More discussion about effective communication can be found in Chapters 5 and 6.

Effective provision

The very diversity described in Chapter 1 that can be seen as the strength of Early Years provision in England, has also led to disagreement about effectiveness. Early Years enthusiasts were, therefore, heartened by the very large-scale Effective Provision of Pre-school Education (EPPE) (Sylva et al., 2003) project. This project tracked the progress and development of around 3,000 children, from three years of age over an extended period. Key findings were that part-time pre-school experience (compared to none), enhanced development in terms of independence, cognitive development, concentration and sociability. Disadvantaged children in particular were seen to benefit. No evidence could be found to support full-time over part-time provision. A direct outcome from EPPE was the later Researching Effective Pedagogy in the Early Years (REPEY) project (Siraj-Blatchford et al., 2002). These researchers collected data that might identify aspects of pedagogy which influence child outcomes. The researchers discovered that the children who made most progress in learning and development, were those that had been offered play-based opportunities that had both curriculum and social learning outcomes offered in settings where these outcomes were seen to be complementary. These children also were shown to have the most positive dispositions to learning. Effective pedagogy was defined as, *both the kind of interaction traditionally associated with the term 'teaching', and the provision of instructive learning and play environments and routines* (Siraj-Blatchford et al., 2002, page 1).

PRACTICAL TASK

Take some time now to begin to familiarise yourself with Appendix 2 Areas of Learning and Development, in the Practice Guidance for the Early Years Foundation Stage (2008). This section is provided to guide practitioners as they 'plan, observe and assess'. What do you notice about the way the six areas of learning are ordered in this section?

Recent research into the development of the brain shows that young children have rapidly developing brains and that this development is supported by immersion in a stimulating environment (Gopnik et al., 1999). Children who are engaged in well-planned play-based learning, where they have the sensitive support of adults, are well placed to make responses to effective stimulation. However, evidence suggests that not all play opportunities are equally stimulating. The Oxford pre-school research (Sylva et al., 1980) found that some play opportunities offered only low yield in terms of learning, and others medium yield, compared to the most effective high yield experiences. When analysed, the high yield experiences that led to intellectual gain were found to have in common;

- clear goals and structure;

- children working in pairs; and

- adults placed in a tutorial role.

You will be aware that children in your setting can sometimes be found playing or working in pairs, but that other groupings may also be evident. Parten (1932) suggested that a child's ability to co-operate with others may be linked to development, beginning with:

- [being] unoccupied or being an onlooker to play;

- parallel play where a child plays alongside rather than with others;

- associative play, where shared action takes place, to co-operative play where roles are proscribed and labour divided.

Given your responsibility to ensure that learning progresses, you will need to consider how you will support the children who find relating to others more difficult.

PRACTICAL TASK

Although play appears to be the natural context in which young children learn, some children may acclimatise less easily to social situations. Make some time to identify a few children who seem to be 'on the fringes' in terms of participating in the setting. What can you find out from these children, and about these children, that may help you to help them to become more engaged in activities and begin to be involved with other children? Make an action plan of the steps you might take and the ways you might make judgements about your success.

The importance of supporting language development

In the sections above, a good deal of research evidence has highlighted the importance of adult support for children's learning. One of the most important aspects of adult support of children's play is in the adult's ability to extend and develop communication, since it is the ability to express thoughts in language that underpins learning. In order to do this effectively, practitioners need to observe sensitively in order to know when to make appropriate interventions. Research shows (Wells, 1986; Tizard and Hughes, 1984; Trevarthan, 1995) that in informal situations adults are highly adept at using language in a manner that supports the young child's development of communication skills. Wells described the way that parents and carers encouraged children to communicate by engaging them in meaningful, context-specific conversation. The topics for conversation needed to be meaningful to the child and the role of the adult was to provide the appropriate structure and feedback. Consider the following interaction between John and his mum:

John's mum is holding him up in her arms to look out through the living–room window. John particularly enjoys this activity so his mum is now able to distract him after a recent fall. John, 17 months, notices that a small tree in his friend's garden has become detached from its stake in the recent high winds, and is now leaning precariously. He points and says, *'Oohh'*.
Following his gaze, his mum describes the situation,
'Oh yes, look, Robert's tree's fallen over in the wind'.
'Fallen over,' John repeats.
'Robert's daddy'll mend it when he comes home, I expect,' his mum suggests.
'Robert's daddy mend it,' John agrees, nodding furiously.

This conversation is repeated many times over the day, sometimes accompanied with John's request to look out of the window, sometimes as a background to other activity. Eventually, John relates, to his grandma that evening, with much enthusiasm and gravity, *'Robert's tree's fallen over. Robert's daddy mend it'*.

At this point, John is able to structure a sentence, employ the correct vocabulary, and communicate effectively with an important person about an issue that is significant to him.

Trevarthan (1995) suggests that the act of communication between young infants and their carers via games such as peak-a-boo, and language play such as nursery rhymes and songs, is evident in all cultures and forms a significant part of enculturation. In contrast, other research by Hughes and Westgate (1997) suggests that adults working in more formal situations appear to be less skilled in this role of language developers, often focusing on checking understanding rather than entering into a genuine conversation in the way of the home situation. They argue that such communication is far less effective in developing language in young learners.

Similarly, returning to the findings in their REPEY research, Siraj-Blatchford et al. (2004) highlight the marked significance of episodes of adults and children entering into periods of engagement in 'reflexive co-construction', which they believe result in learning taking place. The REPEY researchers argue that such periods are dependent on each party 'engaging with the understanding' of the other. The important conditions that need to be in place are:

- the involvement of each party;

- the inclusion of an instructive content.

They label these as episodes of 'sustained shared thinking'. Most significant for you and for your practice is for you to know that one of the conclusions they drew from this large-scale research project was that,

> periods of sustained shared thinking are a necessary prerequisite for the most effective Early Years practice.

> (Siraj-Blatchford et al., 2004)

Interestingly, they found that the most effective context for sustained shared thinking was in child-initiated play, where children were interacting one-to-one with a peer or adult, as these contexts provide the best opportunities for adults to extend children's thinking. Consider the following scenario.

CASE STUDY

It is the first dry day for a week, and in consequence most of the children in the setting have gone outdoors. A group of energetic boys and girls have seized on the wheeled toys and are chasing around the hard-surfaced area at great speed. A second group of children have decided to lay down a blanket, set out some dolls and soft toys and have a picnic. Although initially co-existing peaceably, the children with the vehicles skim by at great speed ever closer to the blanket, sending cups and plates spinning accompanied by loud wails from the picnickers. The wails seem to serve to excite further speed and more daring

continued

---

swerving. *Following several ignored warnings about safety, the practitioner draws the two groups together and suggests they make some suggestions about keeping both groups safe and happy. The children quickly see the need for a physical barrier to demarcate the play space. The 'racers' disappear and return with a canvas windbreak and a mallet. They point out this will also have the benefit of keeping the picnicking families out of the wind. Several attempts to hammer the poles into the hard surface fail. The practitioner, who has been watching from a distance, returns and enquires what the problem is. They discuss the hard surface and the need to drive the posts into something softer like 'when we used it on a trip to the beach', Caspar offers. The practitioner reminds them there is sand in the outdoor pit. The first suggestion of relocating the picnic to the sandpit is greeted by objections from the picnickers who decide they don't want sand in the picnic, and pre-ferred the shady spot under the tree. Several minutes' more discussion about containers resulted in some large pots being sourced, by the practitioner and the children, filled with sand and the windbreak poles being supported in those. Siraj-Blatchford et al. suggest that developing sustained shared thinking is dependent on the adult:*

- *being aware of the child's interests and understanding;*
- *working with the child together to develop an idea or skill;*
- *scaffolding learning and co-constructing meaning;*
- *having an awareness of the nature, quality and frequency of 'adult–child' verbal interactions which are crucial to children's learning.*

The setting in which you are working appears to be giving children little opportunity to initiate their own learning; most of the session is occupied by children being involved in adult-led activity. Who would you talk to about this? What strategies might you try to introduce that could begin to develop good, effective practice?

Seeing connections in learning

The last commitment in the Learning and Development theme is that: *Children learn best through physical and mental challenges* (EYFS, 2008).

Sometimes, those challenges may be presented by adults, or by other children, but chil-dren also need opportunities to discover their own challenges. If this is indeed to happen, this means that they must be allowed to have some control over their learning. Children arriving each day into an environment which is unchanging, and in which their choices are limited in terms of resources, will quickly become stultified and either switch off, or find ways of subverting opportunities to meet, what for them appear to be more inter-esting ends. For example, you will already have noticed that young children find endless challenge in toilet and cloakroom areas if the more closely adult supervised areas prove uninteresting! It is important that you ensure that you present young learners with choices about the way they will spend their time, where they will play, with what, and with whom. If children are always given resources to work with in a particular way, for example with paint always provided in a closed pot, a thick 12" brush and grey sugar paper, they will learn a good deal less about colour, texture and manipulation than if they are given different types of paint, brushes/tools and surfaces on which to work. They will also feel more motivated to investigate, try out new approaches and to make connections in their thinking. By encouraging them to become creative thinkers, practitioners are ensuring young learners are able to be involved in *imaginative activity, fashioned so as to produce outcomes that are both original and of value* (NACCE, 1999).

Some observers are concerned that the repeated government interventions to control what is taught and the way it is taught has impacted negatively on young learners in particular. There has been concern that the drive to raise standards has led to downward pressure in schools to formalise the curriculum for 3 to 5 year olds (Hodson and Keating, 2007). At the same time, building on the NACCE report (1999), *All our futures: Creativity, Culture and Education,* other interested parties have begun to call for greater opportunity to foster creative development in children to ensure that these learners grow into citizens able to develop and extend the world in which they live.

> *The focus of education must be on creating people who are capable of thinking and doing new things, not simply repeating what past generations have done, but equipped for a world of challenge and change.*

> (Fisher and Williams, 2004)

The EYFS Practice Guidance (2008) states:

> *Children's development must be extended by the provision of support for their curiosity, exploration and play.*

As successive governments in the UK, in recent years, have focused on improving children's learning, a particular interest has emerged in the way children 'learn to learn'. Hargreaves (2005) reported that developing research and policy in this area should become a government priority. Similar concerns about effective teaching that promotes learning for all children, are articulated in the 'Gilbert Report' (2006), A *Vision for Teaching and Learning in 2020*, with its focus on personalising learning.

Siraj-Blatchford (2007) extending the findings of the EPPE and REPEY projects on the significance of 'sustained shared thinking' in effective Early Years settings, has since gone on to consider the relationship between creativity, communication and collaboration. Drawing on Vygotsky (2004), she argues that in the past a false dichotomy has been established between learning things and learning what to do with what has been learnt. She states that in actuality the process of constructing meaning draws on all previous experience of the individual, with both imagined experiences and real experiences contributing to this process. To demonstrate this, Siraj-Blatchford cites examples of children's play experience; for example, children observed in a travel agent setting, draw on both the real-life experience of a visit, and the imaginary experiences in their play, to develop their understanding. The use made of a 'credit card', referred to as a cheque, and the discussions surrounding the acquisition of luggage, demonstrate the way the group negotiate meaning through their play. Vygotsky (2004) in Siraj-Blatchford (2007) argues, *A child's play is not simply a reproduction of what he has experienced, but a creative reworking of the impressions he has acquired.* Siraj-Blatchford concludes her argument by stating that Early Years education should now concern itself with an aim to *develop the children's own creative competence* and ensuring that the curriculum *maximises the children's engagement in the process of 'learning to learn'* (ibid).

In well-planned provision, it is the ability for young learners to move between areas and activities that encourages them to begin to make links in their learning. Consider the following.

CASE STUDY

The Nursery class had been following a theme of 'mini-beasts' when one boy, Usman, usually quiet, quite disengaged and making very slow progress in his learning, initiated a worm hunt with Hussain. Armed with spades and buckets from the continuous provision in the sand tray they set about digging away turf in the garden, in a quest to find worms. This endeavour completely captivated their interest and day after day the friends dug for worms. Their enthusiasm for the project was infectious and soon many children were digging. The previously quiet boy began to talk animatedly about worms (and snakes). The practitioners in the setting built on this enthusiasm by providing: magnifying glasses; books; laminated cards to aid identification of species; photographs mounted in the garden to form a talking wall; and worm-shaped writing books. Focused activities featured moving like worms, stories about worms and a video on the role of worms in the growing process, and in the continuous provision, play mats with worms on were used to make long and short model worms.

REFLECTIVE TASK

Using the scenario described above, make some notes under the following headings (taken from the EYFS commitment to Creativity and Critical thinking) that show evidence of opportunities for children to:

- *Make connections;*
- *Transform their understanding;*
- *Be involved in sustained shared thinking.*

If you were working in this setting, what other provision would you make to ensure that Usman and Hussain continue to be involved in highly motivating learning opportunities?

Areas of learning and development

If you are to establish yourself as an effective EYFS practitioner, you will need to spend some time familiarising yourself with this area of the Practice Guidance. You will also find it useful to arm yourself with a book such as *Teaching Early Years Foundation Stage* (Basford and Hodson, 2008), which gives some useful background both for those working towards QTS and to other allied professionals.

Unlike in the Primary National Curriculum, which is based on subject areas arranged hierarchically with core subjects (English, mathematics, science and information communication technology) attracting a greater proportion of the timetable than the foundation subjects (history, geography, art, PE, RE, personal ,health and social education), the areas of Learning and Development in the Practice Guidance are arranged in six equal aspects.

- Personal, Social and Emotional Development (PSED).

- Communication, Language and Literacy (CLLD).

- Problem solving, Reasoning and Numeracy (PRN).

- Knowledge and Understanding of the World (KUW).

- Physical Development.

- Creative Development.

The interesting fact about this arrangement is that all the areas are considered to be equally important, and represent the skills, knowledge and experiences appropriate to babies and young children. The structure of this model of learning is intended to convey the holistic nature of young children's learning; that nothing is compartmentalised, and that everything links.

CHALLENGES and DILEMMAS

How far, in your observations and discussions to date, have you found evidence that the ethos in your setting is one of valuing all areas of learning equally? If you are a student or trainee placed in a primary school setting you may be beginning to question how far practitioners are indeed able to ensure that the holistic ethos of the EYFS practice guidance is maintained. Research such as that presented in the Early Years Learning and Development Review (DCSF, 2009) has highlighted the pressures often experienced in these settings. The emphasis laid on early reading in particular, may be felt to be skewing provision. There is insufficient space in this chapter to discuss these complexities, but this review may help you to extend your understanding of current views on learning in the Early Years.

C H A P T E R   S U M M A R Y

Learning and Development is a vast area which can only be touched on here, however, it is the intention that this chapter will have provided you with an insight into the relationship between the theory and research you are becoming familiar with, and the placement experience you are engaging in. It is recommended that you extend your understanding further by reading some of the material listed below.

Athey, C (1990) *Extending Thought in Young Children.* London: Paul Chapman Publishing.

Basford, J and Hodson, E (eds) (2008) *Achieving QTS: Teaching Early Years Foundation Stage.* Exeter: Learning Matters.

Bruner, J (1978) The Role of Dialogue in Language Acquisition, in Sinclair, AJ *The Child's Conception of Langauage.* New York: Springer-Verlag.

Central Advisory Council for Education (England) (1967) *Children and their Primary Schools.* London: HMSO.

DfES (2007) *The Early Years Foundation Stage Practice Guidance.* Nottingham: DfES.

Donaldson, M (1978) *Children's Minds.* Glasgow: Fontana.

Fisher, R and Williams, M (eds) (2004) *Unlocking Creativity.* London: David Fulton.

Gopnik, A, Melzoff, A and Kuhl, P (1999) *How Babies Think: The Science of Childhood.* London: Weidenfeld and Nicolson.

Hargreaves, D (2005) *About Learning: Report of the Learning Working Group.* Demos.

Hodson, E and Keating, I (2007) The Management and Training Needs of Reception Teachers Working with the Foundation Stage Curriculum. *International Journal of Early Years,* 15(1): March, 65–79.

Hughes, M & Westgate, D (1997) Activities and the Quality of Pupil Talk. *Education 3–13,* 18(2): 41–7.

Moyles, J (1989) *Just Playing?: The Status of Play in Early Childhood Education.* Milton Keynes: Open University Press.

National Advisory Committee on Creative and Cultural Education (1999) *All Our Futures: Creativity,Culture & Education.* Nottingham: DfEE.

Parten, M (1932) Social Participation Among Pre-school Children. *Journal of Abnormal and Social Psychology,* 27: 243–69.

Piaget, J (1955) *The Language and Thought of the Child.* London: Routledge and Kegan Paul.

QCA/DfEE (2000) *Curriculum Guidance for the Foundation Stage.* London: QCA.

Siraj-Blatchford, I (2007) Creativity, Communication and Collaboration: The Identification of Pedagogic Progression In Sustained Shared Thinking. *Asia-Pacific Journal of Research In Early Childhood Education,* Vol 1 (2): 3–33.

Siraj-Blatchford, I, Sylva, K, Muttock, S, Gilden, R and Bell, D (2002) *Researching Effective Pedagogy in the Early Years.* Research Report RR356. Nottingham: DfES.

Sylva, K, Roy, C and Painter, M (1980) *Childwatching at Haygroup and Nursery.* London: Grant McIntyre.

Sylva, K, Melhuish, E, Sammons, P, Siraj-Blatchford,I and Taggart, B (2003) *The Effective Provision of Pre-School Education (EPPE) Project: Findings from the Early Primary Years.* Available online at: www.dcsf.gov.uk/research/data/uploadfiles/SSU SF 2004 02 pdf .

Sylva, K, Siraj-Blatchford, I and Taggart, B (2004) *Assessing Quality in the Early Years: Early Childhood Environment Rating Scale.* Stoke on Trent: Trentham Books.

Tizard, B and Hughes, M (1984) *Young Children Learning.* London: Fontana.

Trevarthan, C (1995) The Child's Need to Learn a Culture. *Children and Society,* 9(1): 5–19.

Vygotsky, L (1978) *Mind in Society: the Devlopment of Higher Psychological Processes.* Cambridge MA: Harvard University Press.

Vygotsky, L (2004) Imagination and Creativity in Childhood. *Journal of Russian and East European Psychology,* 42(1): 4–84.

Wells, G (1986) *The Meaning Makers.* Sevenoaks: Hodder and Stoughton.

Wood, D (1986) Aspects of Teaching and Learning, in M and Light, P *Children of Social Worlds.* Cambridge: Polity Press.

FURTHER READING

Basford, J and Hodson, E (eds) (2008) *Achieving QTS: Teaching Early Years Foundation Stage.* Exeter: Learning Matters.

Evalngelou, M, Sylva, K, Kyriaciu, K, Wild, M and Glenny, G (2009). *Early Years Learning and Development Literature Review.* London: DCFS-RR 176.

Riley, J (ed) (2007) *Learning in the Early Years: A Guide for Teachers of Children 3–7.* London: Paul Chapman.

8 Next steps

Karen Perry

CHAPTER OBJECTIVES

By the end of this chapter you should understand:

- *the consistent and cyclical nature of reflection;*
- *that reflective practice is a way to embed a structural approach to critical evaluation of theory and practice;*
- *how a receptive attitude to the reflective process is an essential tool to develop professional understandings;*
- *the value of reflection as a collaborative pursuit, to support new and improved ways of working;*
- *reflective practice can be used as a mechanism for analysing and challenging established ways of working.*

This chapter addresses the following Professional Standards for EYPS:
EYPS: S38; 39.

Introduction

This final chapter encourages you to take an anticipatory approach in considering the impact of your actual placement experience in terms of your knowledge, skills understanding, and what this means for the next stage of your professional work with children and their families.

You may have now demonstrated the competencies required to gain your relevant professional status, or still have a number of other placement experiences to encounter. Regardless of the particular stage you are at, you are moving from 'becoming' a professional, to 'being' a professional. The issues and challenges you face will change – but the process of reflection will not.

Effective reflective practice

CASE STUDY

A full pathway EYP student expressed her expectations and concerns prior to her first placement as primarily focused upon establishing, good relationships with staff, parents and children...[and to] actually enjoy a placement. *After her five-week experience in an Early Years setting she was given the opportunity to reflect upon these earlier concerns:* It is possible to enter a setting with positivism and achieve an enjoyable experience...staff

continued

are more encouraging and supportive when students show enthusiasm and pleasure to be in the setting, being part of the team is not enough, you need to work at it, see their difficulties but be proactive and supportive in encouraging them to explore possible solutions *(EYPS Student 2009). In terms of the importance of developing a culture of professionalism with reflection at the centre of practice, she also highlighted some of the difficulties she faced:* Encouraging others to look at their practice is difficult, I know how challenging that can be, to be taken out of your comfort zone. I feel that as a student all the time, that's why it's so important to build trust within a team to make others feel that it is a sign of strength to question your practice and that you are there for each other, to offer support rather than judge...but it takes time to develop that kind of relationship which you may not have in all placements *(EYPS Student 2009).*

The comments made by the student demonstrate her identification of elements of practice she considered as both integral and problematic to her goal of obtaining EYP status. Returning to the question of building professional relationships and identifying some of the underlying issues facilitated a powerful opportunity for self-awareness and analysis of what she considered were important factors and served to highlight elements of her practice that she felt were central to her success in future placements.

As Ghaye and Ghaye (1998, page 93) suggest, *It is the ability to see through ... situations and understand the meaning of what is happening* that is at the core of effective reflective practice. The EYP in the case study demonstrated how the process of 'seeing through' a situation requires honesty in order to reflect and learn from new experiences. It is important for you to acknowledge not only your personal skills and achievements, but also your fears and anxieties. This type of self-assessment enabled the student to see beyond the initial issue of building positive relationships with staff and children. As a result, she was able to consider her own behaviour and the responses of others on a broader scale. This will have implications for the way she develops both her own practice and leads and support others in building towards her EYP status.

Getting the most from your critical reflection may not always feel a safe process as questioning practice can be a threatening endeavour. It may be helpful for you to view it in terms of, *being professionally self-critical without being destructive* and indicative of a way of *making sense of professional action* (Ghaye and Ghaye, 1998, page 3). The process of reflection is important in establishing an approach that leads to continued questioning of your actions, interactions and plans, and which serves to support your professional confidence as you gain a better understanding of your practice and pedagogical beliefs. Given the range of opportunities presented during a professional placement and the possible implications for the development of your practice, the idea of reflecting on those experiences in order to inform future action will be a useful endeavour. The opportunity to explore and challenge your own beliefs may also serve to authenticate your practice as you examine your own philosophy and begin to develop your own professional voice.

Reflection and self-evaluation can undoubtedly assist you in your own professional development, however it also has important implications for the way you evaluate and improve the experiences you provide for children. The EYFS (DCSF, 2008a) highlights the part reflective practices have in improving the quality of learning experiences, maintaining a need to *understand and engage in informed reflective practice* (DCSF, 2008, page 9) as a way for you and your colleagues to continually assess and develop provision. The issue of sustaining and improving quality experiences and environments in line with the EYFS and ECM principles is outlined in Early Years Quality Improvement Support Programme (EYQISP, 2008). This guidance maintains the importance of continually engaging with reflective practices and the place it may subsequently have in improving provision and outcomes for children. EYQISP guidance considers reflection as key to, *empowering practitioners to see themselves as learners, seeking improvements in their practice, reducing inequality and narrowing the achievement gap* (DCSF, 2008b, page 6). Therefore, when considering the place of reflection as a tool to develop and question individual understanding, and practice, it is important that you acknowledge its importance in order to embed it as part of your professional role.

The remainder of this chapter is intended to encourage you to consider how reflective practice can support the themes and commitments of the EYFS (2008). It will encourage you to explore your own personal perceptions and beliefs in the light of your placement, and help to make sense of issues that have arisen. One of the challenges of becoming a professional is the way you make sense of theory and policy when framing your own pedagogical practice. Tensions will always arise, whether they are concerned at a micro level with relationships, or at a macro/exo level when you are exploring how policy and legislation is translated into practice.

A unique child

Appreciating the individual ways children develop, acknowledging uniqueness, individual characteristics, interests and learning styles requires your consideration of the complex nature of learning and development. Through your studies you will have begun to appreciate this; however, the opportunity to gain first-hand experience can provide an invaluable context in which to explore the way this knowledge relates to everyday practice within Early Years settings. As Ghaye and Ghaye maintain, "*a blend of practice-with-principle* (1998, page 3) is integral to supporting reflexivity as a consistent element of practice, based on gaining and developing knowledge and skills and reflecting on how they relate to direct experience and your own professional development.

As you listen and respond to the actions of an individual child, you can consider how to go beyond the assessment of the effectiveness of your interaction or the suitability of the resources and experiences you provide, and begin to reflect on the underlying meaning a child may be constructing. By linking experiences and observations to your theoretical understanding of how children develop, including the variation in rate and the range of environmental influences, you will gain a more informed view of where that child is on their learning journey and how best to support them in their next steps. However, Rix (2008) makes a salient point when he maintains the importance of keeping a realistic but open mind to assessing your underpinning knowledge, stating *You cannot understand everything but you can identify possible routes to better practice, possible barriers to engagement and possible means to overcome them* (2008, page 80). Reflecting on how you understand the themes and commitments of the EYFS, assessing successes, addressing challenges and developing possible strategies to overcome them, can serve to deepen your appreciation of the underlying principles in a way that can be viewed as positive learning experience.

While academic investigations may be an important element of obtaining relevant qualifications in the field of Early Years, the complexities of how best to support the individual and unique child require you to be able to rely not only on the knowledge you have but on your ability to continue the process. As previously highlighted, the practice of reflection is one considered as both central and continuous (Ghaye and Ghaye, 1998; Craft and Page Smith, 2008) to professional development. However, in order to support such a process, you will also need to acknowledge the place and importance of continued engagement with pedagogical debates, and as part of this seek out and investigate other views and perspectives, in order to support the continuation of your own learning journey.

Reflecting on her past experience of completing a BA Hons Early Childhood Studies degree and achieving EYP status, a Family Support Worker considered how the opportunities to investigate and critically engage with the theory underpinning her work with children supported her own professional development. *How do you know that a child is meeting their developmental milestones if you don't know the theory behind it? Working in social care keeping up to date with legislation and policy is essential when working with children and families, doing my Early Years degree and Early Years Professional Status was ideal in keeping me on track and helped me ask the right questions* (Family Support Worker 2010).

To keep up to date with current thinking, policy and initiatives, as well as identifying possible gaps in your understanding, can be a daunting as well as time-consuming endeavour, but it has the potential to enhance your own professional experience and that of the children you work with. This skill is also viewed as a key part of professional development for those undertaking EYP status, with the ability to use and *draw on research* as well as that of investigating *other sources of effective practice in order to inform and improve their own and colleagues' practice* (CWDC, page 73, S38), contributing to enhancing personal practice, setting development and leading other professionals.

CHALLENGES and DILEMMAS

Supporting the child in making choices, the provision of sufficient time, and offering the opportunity to explore and develop their own learning, are areas worthy of exploration when you aim to keep the child at the centre of your practice. However, facilitating that in practice can be problematic. Organisation, planning and resourcing can require a great deal of thought in order to ensure individual children are supported in busy settings. The cycle of ongoing observation, assessment and reflection has the potential to support your understanding of achieving this, while also supporting an informed appraisal of the way you need to develop your practice.

How could you develop your practice to ensure you apply what you understand about supporting children's choices? Make some notes highlighting possible sources of information, guidance and support. What implications are there for developing the environment, routine, organisation and support of other professionals?

How would you assess the effectiveness of your provision? What are the issues faced by those in Reception classes in ensuring the unique child is supported? How can these be addressed? What might you do in the future if confronted by these issues?

How could you engage with current thinking and models of effective practice as a continuous element to your practice? Have you considered research or further studies to Masters Level?

Positive relationships

Your placement experience offers the opportunity to work as part of a community of professionals. The importance of developing respectful relationships with colleagues, acknowledging their skills and perspectives, is highlighted in the EYFS as key to ensuring the child is at the centre of your practice. Your role in supporting multiple perspectives can also enable the creation of a more informed and holistic picture of the child, as you and your colleagues work together with the child and family.

Through seeking the opinions of others on areas of concern or interest you can create opportunities to elicit new perspectives that may question *your* assumptions or lead you to new avenues of enquiry. As Rix suggests, this serves to *reframe* (2008, page 81) an issue, allowing you to investigate whether others share or contest your views. Opening up reflective discussions and remaining receptive to the perceptions of others, offers the opportunity not only to demonstrate how you value their individual perspective, but also to develop a sense of a shared understanding. As Loughran (2006) suggests, individual involvement in considering an issue can sometimes make it difficult to *step back from the situation* (2006, page 49). However, eliciting the views of colleagues who may not be so directly involved can offer multiple fresh perspectives, which may assist in developing new understandings and in reframing issues.

An EYP student reflected on her concern regarding how she had dealt with challenging behaviour in her placement. She identified some future actions as:

- *a need to become familiar with setting policy; and*
- *to observe how other staff dealt with situations.*

Although initially this seemed a satisfactory course of action it raised other issues for her. She began to consider what constituted challenging behaviour in this setting, and how this reflected or contested with her personal perceptions of acceptability. She began to

continued

reflect on the problematic nature of developing strategies, and on the problematic nature of bringing together and valuing the multiple perspectives of colleagues in order to reach the consensus. She also considered the issue of how such a system reflects and supports the values held by the families and children. Through engagement with these issues firstly on a personal level, and then collaboratively, as she discussed them with her placement colleagues, she was able to gain an insight into her own understandings and appreciate the importance of engaging in professional debate in order to ensure all those involved understood and consistently implemented the policy. The process also served to highlight the importance of finding ways to include different perspectives and support the questioning and reassessment of the team views on behaviour. At the same time they were able to evaluate value judgements, the construction of policies and communication with children and parents.

At this point it may be helpful to consider not only the value of recognising the usefulness of using the perspectives of colleagues but recognising the significance of the wider workforce and the differing ways they may construct the same child. Reflecting on her first experience of involvement in the CAF process Jayne, a Family Support Worker, acknowledged the convergence of perspectives as, *like a jigsaw*. Views of the child were presented by those with medical, educational and family support backgrounds, each framed by their own professional ideology, which impacted on the way they saw the strengths and needs of the child. She considered how each perspective, when brought together, gave her a valuable opportunity to *see more of the whole child*. This was a valuable opportunity, and subsequently served to inform the support she was then able to offer. It also enabled her to develop an appreciation of the way *other professionals can view the same child in very different ways*. Although the CAF process is a very specific one, the salient point for you as a professional may be in the value of developing a professional ethos that takes account of such multiple perspectives. Through developing your own appreciation of multiple perspectives and acknowledging the importance of a holistic view of the child, you have the opportunity to look beyond your own professional agenda and see the child within the wider social context.

The value of utilising those around you to explore your own perceptions and understandings – whether a colleague, mentor or critical friend – may well be one familiar to you; indeed, Craft and Page Smith maintain that *reflection demands that we create opportunities to bounce ideas off others* (2008, page 22). This may be a recognisable element of reflective practice but it also continues to be of value as you develop as a professional; in promoting the exchange of knowledge and ideas, the clarification of understandings, valuing multiple perspectives and enabling the co-construction of meaning. However, this in itself can be problematic, as it may lead you to identify gaps in your own experience and consider how best to develop a strategy that address them.

Sarah, a QTS student, expressed concern about how she could develop relationships with parents during her placement. Although aware of the importance of facilitating parents as partners, as espoused in the EYFS (2008), she recognised both her lack of experience and of confidence to undertake appropriate action. While acknowledging the challenges of time and opportunity to establish herself as part of the school team, and of developing effective communication with parents and carers, she was keen to develop her own role and her professional skills in this area. Using her weekly review meetings with her school mentor she was able to share her concerns and develop an action plan. This involved observing and reflecting on how staff interacted with parents in order to develop positive, friendly, but professional relationships. Weekly discussions then enabled the setting of realistic targets based on creating opportunities both informal at the beginning and end of the school day to exchange information face to face, and formally, through shared written records.

Utilising regular opportunities to discuss and review her experiences nurtured Sarah's growing self-confidence and skills and led to the identification of possible next steps. Having the courage and the self-awareness to acknowledge deficits in experience, as Sarah did, resulted in an opportunity to create a positive learning experience. Her openness and desire to address what she felt was a barrier to her professional development, resulted not only in the building of her own skills and confidence but also in the opening of a professional dialogue between herself and her mentor in which they were able to explore their understanding and perceptions of effective communication.

REFLECTIVE TASK

Consider an area of practice that you feel least confident about.

- *How could a mentor or critical friend support you with addressing this issue?*
- *How could this process be facilitated?*
- *How could the development of an action plan be of use to you?*
- *How would discussion help you and other professionals develop a better shared understanding?*

If you consider developing an appreciation of the roles and perspectives of other professionals may be an important element in developing an understanding of the child and their family, how can you ensure that you facilitate this in your own professional development?

Enabling environments

The process of using observations to reflect on children's experiences, learning and development is central to practitioners in the Early Years sector. The implications for you as a professional lie in developing your ability to make links between theory and practice. Equally important is the influence on your subsequent actions. As the EYFS states: *Without observation, overall planning would simply be based on what we felt was important, fun or interesting…but might not necessarily meet the needs of the children in our care* (DCSF, 2007, page 1).

By investigating how different contexts, events and situations have implications for children's learning experiences, you can gain a valuable insight into how your provision may support and enable the individual in their learning. However, this can be a time-consuming process which will require the use of planned opportunities for you to critically reflect on the environment you create and on the learning opportunities you provide. Aligned with this is the need to remain open minded to any issues you may uncover by reflecting on how best to take a fresh and honest approach to evaluating something you may well be very familiar with. If utilising planned opportunities to explore aspects of your practice or provision merely serve to reaffirm established thinking, the value of initiating such a process may well be questionable. When reviewing how your environment may be working to support children's learning, you have to consider how you might respond with subsequent action that supports development, rather than by a justification of what you provide.

CASE STUDY

Considering how children operated within a setting was a useful starting point for Julia, a teacher working in a nursery class as part of her involvement in the Effective Early Learning (EEL) project. With her team she was investigating how children used different learning areas of the nursery. They also focused on the role of the adults in supporting independence and autonomy. Through planned observations they were able to identify that few children or adults visited the maths area or used the resources stored there. When discussing their findings Julia and her colleagues reflected on their roles and how their own preferences and interests may have influenced where they had located themselves during sessions. As a team they recognised how they continually supported the creative, outdoor, writing and construction play activities, but the maths area in which they were less interested or confident in, was hardly ever chosen to work in. Further investigation reflected in the less creative way materials were set out or displayed in this area. They considered the way this may have influenced children's views of this area as less important and less highly valued by the adults around them.

Observation and reflections served to highlight issues that neither Julia nor her staff were previously aware of and then to develop a course of action to address them. Planning opportunities for adults to spend time in the area encouraged children to join them and explore the resources. They also planned to reorganise the maths area with children, and develop interactive displays to reinvigorate the space. For you as a practitioner, this may demonstrate the problematic nature of reliance on reflection to address issues you have already identified, as this may fail to bring to the fore other underlying problems.

Reflection

Chak (2006) poses an interesting question, asking if the identification or awareness of a problem is the dominant starting point for reflection, *would there be situations where* 'problems' may not be recognised but reflection is still called for? (Chak, 2006, page 31). This, Chak considers, may stem from a lack of appreciation of how individual personalities, values, and habitual behaviours influence interpretation of effective practice. Therefore, this raises the issue, if you are comfortable with your everyday practice does this have the potential to mask misconceptions and misunderstandings? The importance of reflecting on personal beliefs and the way they may shape your view of effective practice and influence areas for development, therefore, appears worthy of exploration.

REFLECTIVE TASK

- Consider instances during placement experiences that have required elements of reflective practices. Do they reflect problem-orientated situations or are they instances that stem from personal questioning or reflections?
- How could you as a practitioner ensure self-awareness is developed as a way to identify possible biases?
- If an effective tool in seeking to understand personal practice is to reflect on what you do and why you respond in particular ways, how could a journal support this process?

CHALLENGES and DILEMMAS

Using reflection to question practice in a way that investigates the ethos of a workplace or application of policies is a way of exploring the possible differences between the rhetoric and reality of practice. However, the challenge appears to be in developing a methodology that maintains this as both positive and constructive. Ensuring assessment and analysis is viewed, maintained and continuously developed to support quality provision rather than become a destructive and demoralising force, can be a problematic but important issue to address.

Consider how you could:

- use observations to support or question the way policies affect the experiences of children;
- reflect on the way the ethos and policies of a setting are upheld, and the sort of strategies you could use to ensure colleagues are supported in any resulting action.

How could:

- a collegiate approach to the review and development of policies support this as a positive experience?
- you establish a realistic view of your own practice in this area?
- you utilise such an exercise to build confidence within a team?

Learning and development

The use of observation and analysis to support children's active learning maintains the holistic nature of all six areas of Learning and Development and is considered to be central to planning and providing effective experiences and environments (EYFS, 2008). Through the evaluative process you can consider information that enables you to support the interests and skills of the child. Utilising your reflective skills will serve to ensure you explore not only the behaviour you see, but also allow you to consider how to support each child in exploring and developing their own enquiries, making connections in their learning, and offering experiences that challenge and extend thinking.

CHALLENGES and DILEMMAS

The opportunity to discuss practice can have obvious value when considering the chance this presents to share interpretations, offer different perspectives, pool information and develop practice. Logistically this can be problematic; no matter how laudable the intentions, the reality of gathering together those involved – colleagues, parents and the child – can be fraught with difficulty. How you address such issues by making sufficient time and opportunity to ensure others can contribute, will in itself require careful consideration. The information gained through this daily involvement and the understandings constructed as a result, may impact on your response to children's learning.

REFLECTIVE TASK

The process of reflection, although key to interpreting what you see, and identifying what you do next, can present issues for time management and organisation. In order to embed it as part of your routine and to create systematic ways of considering a child's achievements, consider the following.

- *How would you ensure you built in time and opportunity to reflect on your observations? Considering your placement experience to date, what are the effective strategies you may be able to transfer to your future practice?*
- *How could you organise sufficient time for you and your colleagues to share information and reflection? How would you include the child and parents in this process?*
- *How would you ensure your planning has sufficient flexibility to allow you to respond to new understanding?*

The opportunity to experience practice within a variety of Early Years contexts and to reflect on specific themes and commitments contained within the EYFS provides valuable food for thought. Supporting children's active learning, providing opportunities for them to engage with ideas, events or concepts in a way that is both supportive and challenging can present difficulties for you as a practitioner. This may require you to consider how you, your setting and your colleagues support and facilitate children's independence and autonomy and to consider what that may look like in practice. Facilitating children's engagement as they create new and perhaps unorthodox solutions requires the development of an understanding which supports, values and facilitates it as an important aspect of the way children develop their thinking.

> REFLECTIVE TASK
>
> *The opportunity to reflect on aspects of your practice and critically analyse how you value and implement them can often require you to ask sometimes difficult and challenging questions, but through this process you can begin to explore ways of ensuring you are evaluating and re-evaluating how and why you act as you do.*
>
> - *Consider your views on active learning, what does it mean to you? How do you facilitate it?*
> - *How do you communicate its importance to colleagues and parents? How do you demonstrate its value to children?*
> - *Do you impose limitations to active learning and the creative thought processes through your own expectations?*
> - *Do your desired outcomes restrict or facilitate children's learning opportunities?*
> - *How do you ensure children's idea and interests remain central to your planning?*
> - *Can you do this effectively for all the children?*

When considering how you develop your practice, think about how you provide experiences that build on what you see. How do your plans offer challenging opportunities to take learning forward? The consistent cyclical nature of reflective practice may appear to be a familiar model both within your own experience and in the guidance that supports your work in the Early Years. However, it is perhaps equally important to remain open to the prospect that it may lead you to new ways of understanding rather than serving to confirm what you already believe. Reflection in this context considers your role as one which is both continuous and active as you construct new understandings from what you see and do. As Ghaye and Ghaye (1998) maintain it has the potential to support your *ability to construct a professional world that is meaningful* to you (1998, page 122). The idea that through reflection you can claim to be able to find all the answers to the complex issues that affect you as a professional or come to truly know yourself appears to indeed be an unachievable goal. However, if you consider reflection as a *commitment, willingness and enthusiasm to question the knowledge that is created, to challenge personal and collective values and to interrogate the contradictions and paradoxes that appear from the constructions of teachers' professional knowledge* (Ghaye and Ghaye, 1998, page 122), there is considerable value in embedding it as a vital part of your own attempt, if not to find answers, to ask the right questions of yourself and your practice.

CHAPTER SUMMARY

In this chapter we have looked at how reflective activity can support a greater understanding of practice. We have considered the benefits self-analysis can present as you apply the theoretical knowledge and the opportunities it gives to continue engagement with research and current views of effective practice. Viewing the process of reflection as a collaborative pursuit allows reframing and fresh insights. Through reflection we have considered encouraging the development of new ways of working through the exchange of ideas, information and knowledge – supporting not only your own development but that of your colleagues. Although analysing the how and why you act as you do can challenge long-held beliefs and create uncertainties, we have explored the positive aspects of being honest and remaining open-minded. Finally, we have acknowledged that reflection can be both stimulating and liberating for you as you move yourself and your practice forward.

REFERENCES

Chak, A (2006) Reflecting on the Self: An Experience in a Preschool. *Reflective Practice*, 7(1): 31–41.

Children's Workforce Development Council (CWDC) (2008) *Guidance to the Standards for the Award of Early Years Professional Status*. Leeds: CWDC.

DCSF (2007) Effective Practice: Observation, Assessment and Planning, in *Early Years Foundation Stage*. Nottingham: DCSF.

DCSF (2008a) *The Early Years Foundation Stage*. Nottingham: DCSF.

DCSF (2008b) Early Years Quality Improvement Support Programme. Nottingham: DCSF.

Ghaye, A and Ghaye, K (1998) *Teaching and Learning through Critical Reflective Practice*. London: David Fulton.

Loughran, J (2006) A Response to 'Reflecting on the self'. *Reflective Practice*, 7(1): 43–53.

Paige-Smith, A and Craft, A (eds) (2008) *Developing Reflective Practice in the Early Years*. Maidenhead: Open University Press.

Rix, J (2008) Inclusion and Early Years Settings: What's Your Attitude?, in Paige-Smith, A and Craft, A (eds) *Developing Reflective Practice in the Early Years*. Maidenhead: Open University Press.

FURTHER READING

Moyles, J (2006) *Effective Leadership and Management in the Early Years*. Maidenhead: Open University Press.

Nurse, A (2007) *The New Early Years Professional Dilemmas and Debates*. Oxon: David Fulton.

Robins, A (2006) *Mentoring in the Early Years*. London: Paul Chapman.

Whalley, M (2008) *Leading Practice in Early Years Settings*. Exeter: Learning Matters.

Index

toddler room 6
theory and practice 20–1
treasure baskets 89
Trevarthan, C. 64, 101, 102
trips 52, 54
Tutaev, Belle 7
tweenies 6

under-threes 89–90
unique child 20, 47–60, 111–13

visual sweep 99
Vygotsky, L. 26, 40, 98, 104

Wallace, D. 27
Walton, A. 39
welfare requirements 6–7, 34
Wenger, E. 26–7, 33, 34
Westgate, D. 102
wet nurses 3
Wolfendale, S. 69
Wood, D. 26, 98–9

Zimitat, C. 26–7
Zone of Proximal Development (ZPD) 40, 98